MW00800928

Alpine Style

Bringing Mountain Magic Home

Bringing Mountain Magic Home

Alpine Style

KATHRYN O'SHEA-EVANS

Gibbs Smith

Switzerland's Drei Berge Hotel, owned and designed by Paris-based Ramdane Touhami.

For my husband, James, who helps me up every mountain. And for our perfect son, Guy—the reason we climb at all.

First Edition
28 27 26 25 24 5 4 3 2 1

Published by
Gibbs Smith
570 N. Sportsplex Dr.
Kaysville, Utah 84037

1.800.835.4993 orders
www.gibbs-smith.com

Designer: Amy Sly, The Sly Studio
Art director: Ryan Thomann
Editor: Juree Sondker
Production editor: Virgina Snow
Production manager: Felix Gregorio

Printed and bound in China.

Library of Congress Control Number: 2024930922
ISBN: 978-1-4236-6569-4

This product is made of FSC®-certified and other controlled material.

Slim Aarons earned a Purple Heart for combat photography in World War II before becoming a glitterati mainstay. Here he captures the buzzing après-ski scene under the 14,692-foot-high Matterhorn in Zermatt, in 1968.

CONTENTS

INTROD

Isabella Bird was sick, as spent and exhausted as a Victorian-era travel writer could be. And in 1873, doctors felt there was only one way for her to go to cure her ennui: *up.* To the mountains. More specifically, to Colorado, where they believed the region's dry alpine air and sunny disposition would be an instant balm.

It worked. Like so many others in the nineteenth century, Bird revived herself riding through Colorado's ridges on horseback, later publishing her adventures (and details of a purported love affair with a one-eyed Irish expat and fur trapper, Jim Nugent), in her book *A Lady's Life in the Rocky Mountains*. One hundred and forty-four years later and hot on her heels, I had the same rebirth, minus the steed—and I brought my own stud.

When my husband, James, and I finally decamped sea-level New York City for the Front Range after ten years, my shoulders instantly dropped. Suddenly I was no longer a weary New Yorker mired in Midtown's fog. I was a ski bunny, in all seasons, bounding through wildflower-strewn meadows in summer and slinking down powdered sugar-frosted

OPPOSITE: Snuggled in Givenchy, Audrey Hepburn films a scene from 1963's *Charade* on location at the Megève ski slopes in the Rhône-Alpes. Watch it; it's been deemed "the best Hitchcock movie Hitchcock never made."

But if I sound like I'm romanticizing it, I'm not.

I WOULDN'T BLAME YOU FOR ROLLING YOUR

Former combat photographer Slim Aarons devoted his postwar life largely to "photographing attractive people doing attractive things in attractive places." In 1963 Gstaad, that meant ski bunnies in repose.

VACATIONLANDS for the glitterati

slopes come December. No wonder Aspen, Vail, and Telluride have become de facto vacationlands for the glitterati. The air is so dry in Colorado that the snowflakes often look like they were cut from paper: filigreed and enormous, the span of an eyelash on my glove. In summer, the mountain air is rich with the scent of subalpine fir and Engelmann spruce. Who needs air freshener?

I wouldn't blame you for rolling your eyes. If I sound like I'm romanticizing it, I'm not. Even the thick, corpulent rodents that scurried past us in Manhattan are replaced here by cotton-tailed rabbits holding jamborees in the fields. Our Christmas trees, too, have been upgraded—no longer the dehydrated options imported to a pockmarked city sidewalk but towering eleven-foot versions we cut ourselves with a twenty-dollar permit from the Forest Service (a tree they'd have to cut down anyway as a forest fire prevention measure). One year, our Christmas tree kept on growing, sending out fresh green shoots from the tip of each branch—right there in our living room. I think she was happy to be so warm and watered. *C'était magique!*

What can I say . . . mountains literally take things up a notch. In an alpine landscape, whether you live in the Adirondacks or Cascades, the Hida Mountains of Japan or the Peruvian Andes, the interior design must, too. If I've learned one thing as a design and travel journalist—interviewing professional decorators and staying in carefully curated hotels on assignment—it's that, like food, decor tastes the best when it's local. Nobody wants to check into a chalet room in St. Moritz only to find it looks transplanted from an airport hotel in Des Moines.

I put that lesson to use at our modern vacation home, Skytop Mountain House, that my husband and I run as a short-term rental in Bailey, Colorado, an hour's drive from our primary home in the Denver suburbs. At nearly ten thousand feet in elevation, mountain life at the house demands a level of coziness and reverence for the landscape year-round. After all, our neighbors up there include black

ABOVE: Frank Sinatra and Dionne Warwick cozied up at a Lake Tahoe, California, ski resort in 1970. I'm slightly obsessed with her sweater.

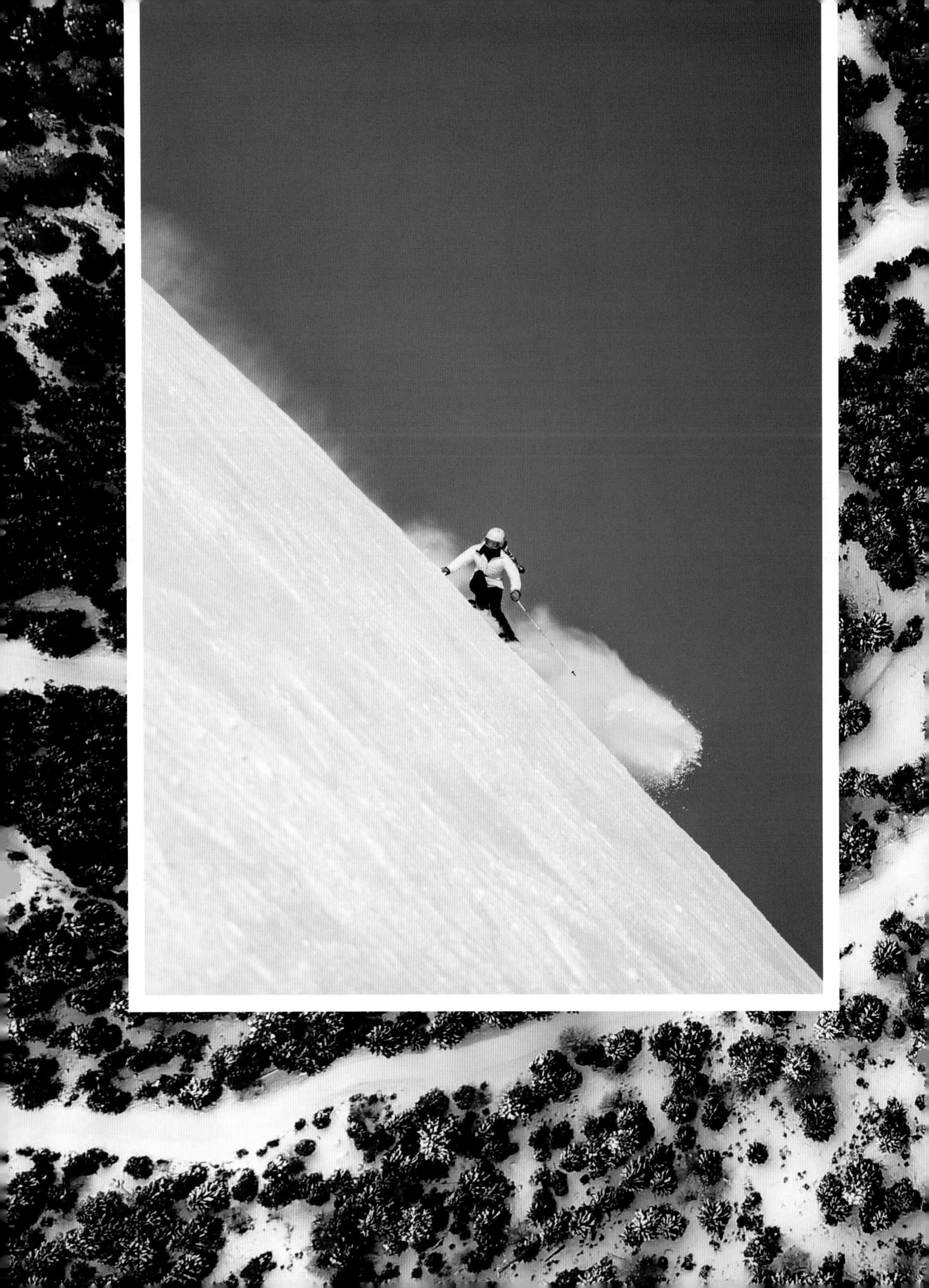

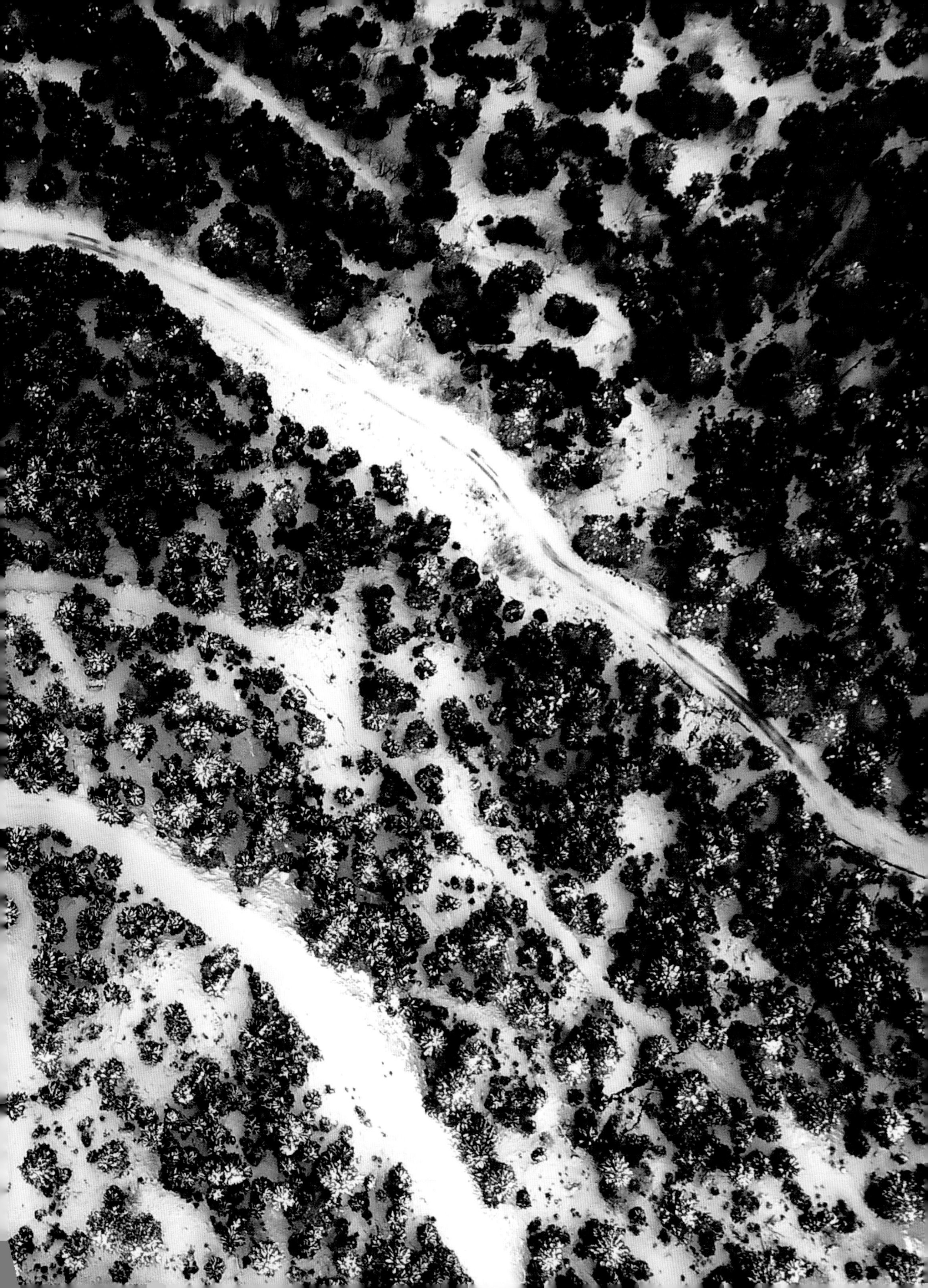

bear, a green-eyed silver fox with a white-tipped tail, and a chipmunk I've nicknamed Chippy that often perkily greets us upon arrival. Wagon-wheel tables and antler chandeliers wouldn't have done us any favors! So in lieu of hackneyed art, we hung photos of Swiss chalets, the buzzing ski lifts of Big Sky, and 1960s *Vogue* supermodels on the slopes.

I took *Friends* character Rachel Green's ill-fated 1994 trip to Vail as my design muse for the house. Nubby bouclé, cinnamon velvet, and saddle-hued leather upholster much of the furniture, all of which we got Fiber-Sealed, a professionally sprayed-on method of stain prevention. (We rent out the house when we're not using it, but even if we didn't, we would still have put in hard-wearing finishes. Delicate is for a buttery *krumkake*, not mountain life!). Even the books are mountain inspired, including Robert Redford's 1978 *The Outlaw Trail*, for which he traced Butch Cassidy's routes through the Old West (mountains have always had a siren call for outlaws), and the photographer Lisa Eisner's *Rodeo Girl* (1999). For a lackluster ground-floor bedroom, I framed pages I ripped out of a 1950s Colorado tour book; in the kids' room, James built a cabin-themed trundle bed and topped it with Pendleton's Glacier National Park blankets. Guests tell us repeatedly that the resulting spaces are welcoming and warm and thoroughly of their place. That Rachel Green might feel right at home is just a bonus!

OPPOSITE: Compared to former mining boomtowns like Aspen, Vail is practically a new build—founded in 1966. But the town worked hard to whip up a storybook Bavarian village feel, which I captured on a recent visit. My takeaway? You can never have too many decorative gables.

To me, true "Alpine style" is not modern and cold—it's more of a Ralph Lauren fever dream sprung to life. And an element of fun is necessary. Mountains have a sense of humor, as anyone who has watched a baby mountain goat try to gambol over shale knows. So I spend many late nights poking around on eBay for the types of vintage finds that, when placed in a sleek and modern shadow-box frame, would up the cool factor, like a 1980s ski sweater or a ski-lift ticket from 1960s Aspen.

I still love the flatlands. I am the child and grandchild of midwestern stock, so the prairies are in my blood, rolling endlessly to the horizon. But they'd be nothing without the juxtaposition of a jagged peak: a climbing challenge dotted with wildflowers and wilder fauna. Thankfully, interior designers and architects from across the globe are up to the task and have illuminated the best of modern and chalet-style alpine living. That's what this book is: an ode to bringing the very best mountain vibes home, from your decor to how you live there from season to season. I recommend thumbing through it by the fire, après-ski or après-hike alike. Just add a hot toddy. ◆

OPPOSITE: **Iglu-Dorf Zermatt, a restaurant and bar at nearly 9,000 feet above sea level in Switzerland, created a perfect après-ski perch in this igloo with a banquette built right into the snow and a "window" that echoes the shapely 14,692-foot spire of the Matterhorn.**

Fall

A Californian hilltop home in the foothills of the Santa Ynez Mountains by Brandon Architects and Patterson Custom Homes captures the spirit of West is Best.

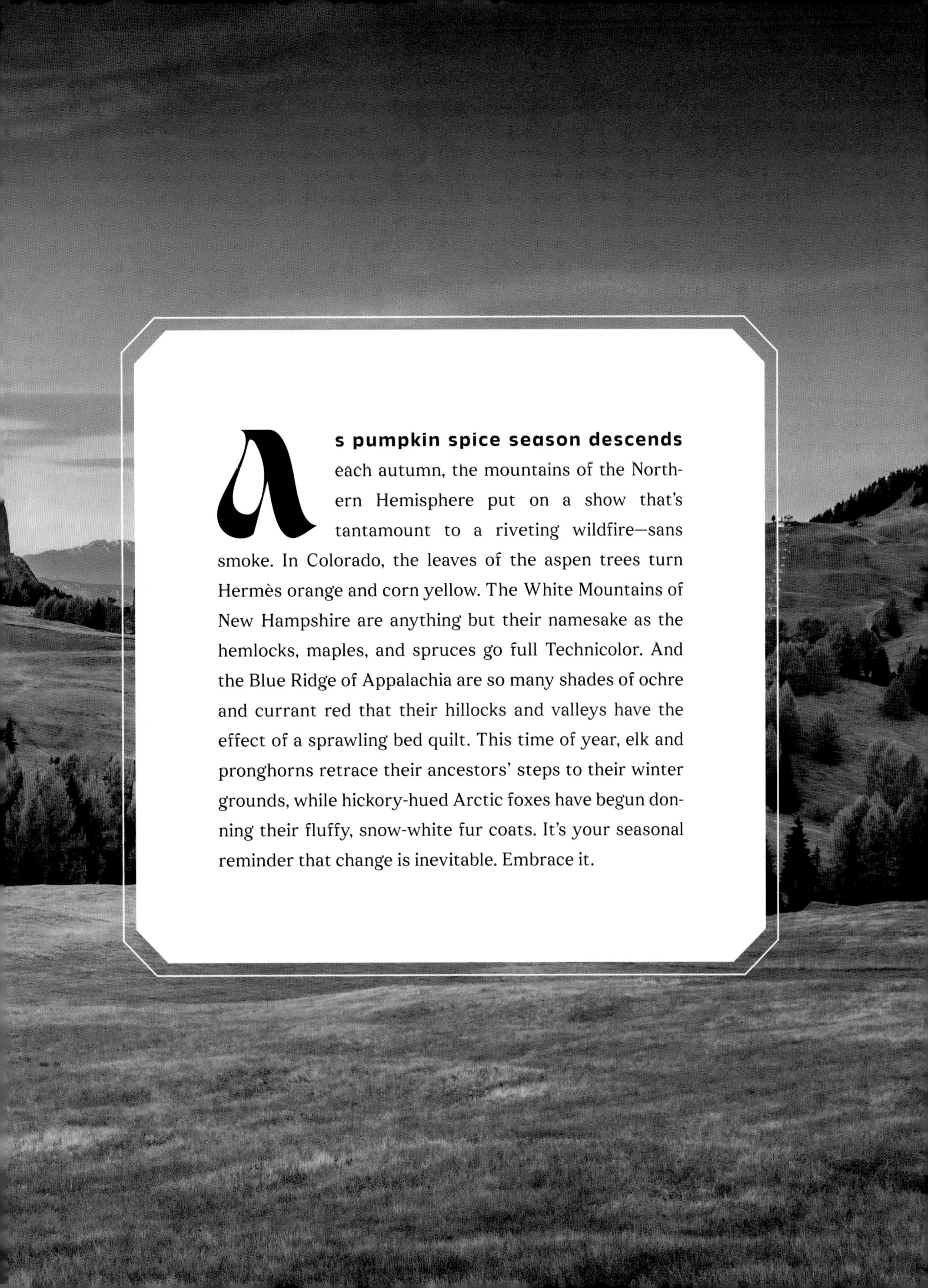

As **pumpkin spice season descends** each autumn, the mountains of the Northern Hemisphere put on a show that's tantamount to a riveting wildfire—sans smoke. In Colorado, the leaves of the aspen trees turn Hermès orange and corn yellow. The White Mountains of New Hampshire are anything but their namesake as the hemlocks, maples, and spruces go full Technicolor. And the Blue Ridge of Appalachia are so many shades of ochre and currant red that their hillocks and valleys have the effect of a sprawling bed quilt. This time of year, elk and pronghorns retrace their ancestors' steps to their winter grounds, while hickory-hued Arctic foxes have begun donning their fluffy, snow-white fur coats. It's your seasonal reminder that change is inevitable. Embrace it.

The WFH life gets an inspiration boost from the forty verdant acres beyond the doors of this Durango, Colorado, home. The homeowner enlisted Massucco Warner to nod to the favored colors of the region's Indigenous people (the Southern Ute Indian Reservation is nearby). The woven tribal blanket hung behind the antique desk is vintage.

OPPOSITE: A plush banquette gives a breakfast nook the comfort of the town diner. Shintaffer continued this one across the entire expanse of windows, which makes it beckon all the more.

ABOVE In Big Sky, Montana, designer Kylee Shintaffer designed the ultimate outdoor living room by bringing indoorsy things out: hurricane lanterns, throws aplenty, even nubby bouclé upholstery.

Indoors, I always take inspiration from the grizzly bear, whose fur coat isn't enough to keep her from hitting snooze until spring. In short, I try to make our home as warm as possible, and quick. On the first of November each year, I pumpkin-spice my life, pulling out our plaid Portuguese flannel bed linens and ordering candles that make our house smell like a morning on an apple farm. (Yes, this is #basic. But it's basic like pearls with timeworn denim are basic. Some things never get evicted from the style rotation for a reason!) Swapping out summer throw blankets for something cuddlier—like a fringed wool in the easy-to-live-with hues of a Burberry trench coat—and cutting some fiery fall foliage branches can be all you need to transform the living room.

Set within a former ghost town in the outskirts of Telluride, Colorado, Dunton Hot Springs constructed the bath house using beams from the original circa 1885 miner bathhouse. You can ogle century-old graffiti as you dip in the 103-degree pool, fed by mineral-rich natural hot springs.

"coziness" by whatever you call it

• • •

GEMÜTLICHKEIT

or

CWTCH

• • •

is really key in autumn.

OPPOSITE: The view walking toward the saloon at Dunton Hot Springs is of 14,165-foot El Diente, an iconic Colorado 14er within the Wilson Range that inspired the Coors logo.

OPPOSITE: I love a tucked-away bed; they feel so much more restful. Designer Tammy Connor placed this one under the exposed hickory-wood beams of this cottage at Blackberry Farm in Tennessee; the two levels of symmetrical curtains soften the effect and juxtapose beautifully beside the turned wood chair.

The concept of hygge became overplayed in recent years, but "coziness" by whatever you call it—be it the Austrian *gemütlichkeit* or Welsh *cwtch*—is really key in autumn. Snuggliness is imperative this time of year, given rapidly undressing tree branches and incoming squalls. To achieve it, diminutive patterns are all but required—from houndstooth to fair isle. Plaids in muted colors also suit autumn perfectly; they've always given me a back-to-campus feeling. It's nice to use a fabric with meaning to you and your ancestors, whether a madras from Chennai, India, or a Scottish wool tartan, worn since the third century CE and available in hundreds of motifs designed for varying surnames. Toss a few plaid pillows around and—*pouf*—you've summoned the autumn equinox.

In the kitchen, I stock the cupboards in early September with everything I need to make autumnal delights with our son, Guy, on a Sunday whim: cinnamon, nutmeg, and vanilla; brown sugar; bottomless flour; and Gala apples, which I buy for their name alone. I pull out all the woolen stocky sweaters I can find from their roost in storage. The trees are putting on a show . . . isn't it time we did, too? ◆

To maximize the kaleidoscopic greens of the Wasatch Mountains beyond this Deer Valley, Utah, terrace, Massucco Warner kept the palette of the outdoor furniture sedate in stone grays. Texture and more texture—rock, rattan, and stone—echo the alpine landscape.

ABOVE: Rumor has it that stands of quaking aspen trees are connected by their roots underground—making them the largest organisms on the planet.

OPPOSITE: The only animal I love more than a horse is a horse with great hair.

FALL CHALET TOUR

Jackson Hole, Wyoming

◆

A nine-thousand-square-foot house facing the 13,775-foot-tall peak of Grand Teton could easily feel cavernous and cold, but not in the hands of the Chicago architect Celeste Robbins of Robbins Architecture. Here, the author of *The Meaningful Modern Home: Soulful Architecture and Interiors* has maximized the panorama of the floor-to-ceiling windows while giving the interior the warmth of a Frank Lloyd Wright bolt-hole, all exposed Douglas fir beams and rough stone, a scroll-arm velvet sofa by the fire.

MAXIMIZED THE PANORAMA OF

FLOO WS W

GIVI WAR

OF A WRIG

BOLT MAK

BEAM STO

SCROLL-ARM VELVET SOFA BY T

PREVIOUS: Clean-lined stone and wood are an ideal juxtaposition for nature's grandeur. I love that in this Robbins sitting area, the floor-to-ceiling window framing and built-ins essentially turn that TV screen into an afterthought.

ABOVE: A home with a low and clean profile, such as this one by Celeste Robbins of Robbins Architecture, allows the flourish of the surrounding mountains to be the star.

PREVIOUS: Mountain rooms really need a rustic touch—just a bit—to suit the landscape. I have an expensive infatuation with hand-carved Tyrolean chairs (seen in the corner of this sitting room at Le Coucou). They're fairy tales in seat form, and look dynamite next to plush upholstered pieces.

ABOVE: A custom scalloped headboard seems to mirror the mountains—albeit in a thoroughly modern way—at Le Coucou, a slopeside hotel in Méribel, France.

OPPOSITE: Le Coucou's interiors were designed by architectural designer Pierre Yovanovitch and nod to the locale. Designed in 1883, this pattern by William Morris is cheekily named The Strawberry Thief and depicts thrushes that flourish in Méribel—and which absconded with the fruit in his country house in Oxfordshire.

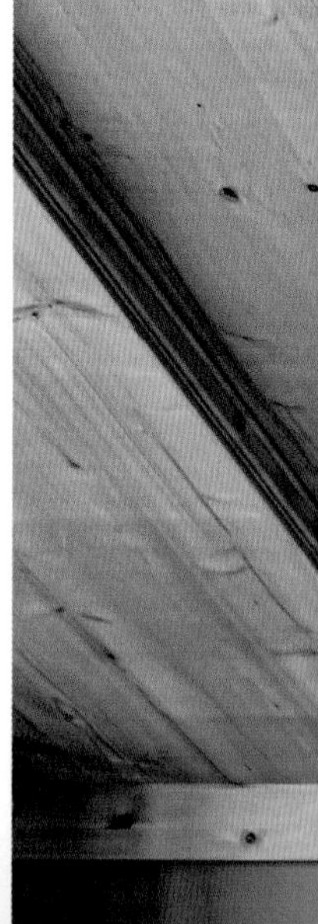

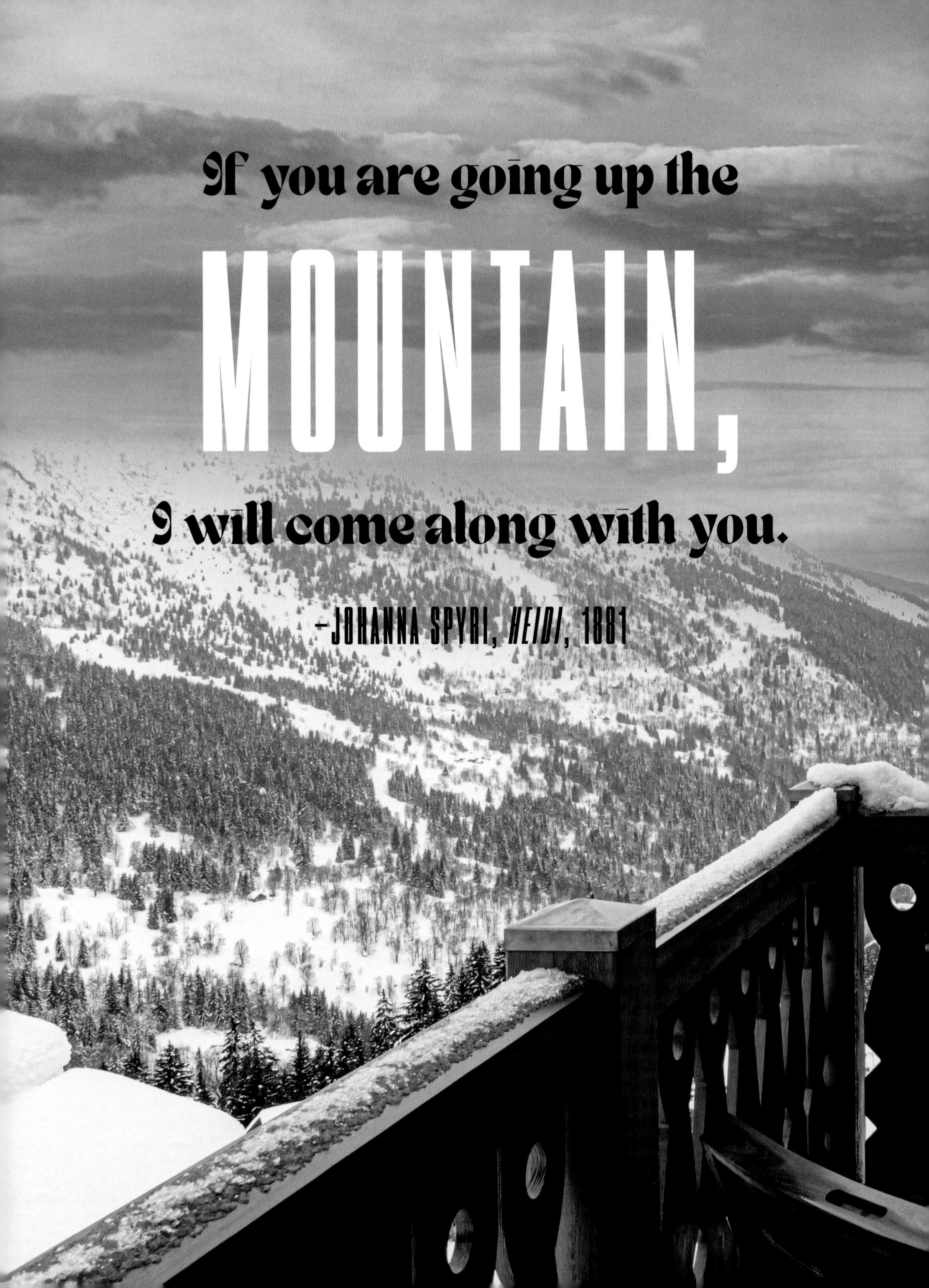
If you are going up the
MOUNTAIN,
I will come along with you.
–JOHANNA SPYRI, HEIDI, 1881

Le Coucou

LEFT: It's almost physically impossible to not relax into this snaking corner sofa at Le Coucou, especially because of its low-slung profile and deep bottom cushion.

ABOVE: Deep overhanging eaves, carved balusters, and wood aplenty—from larch to pine—are hallmarks of Alpine chalets that Le Coucou put to beautiful use on this terrace that peeps out on the snowdusted peaks.

FOLLOWING PAGE: Paris architect Fabrizio Casiraghi had a delectable muse when designing the Experimental Chalet in Verbier, including the rich saturated colors of sorbet. Pressed local plants are framed and tucked above the wall paneling here, while the mirrors bounce needed light around.

FRENCHIE
VERBIER
ENTRÉES
BURRATA
poire, granola & curry de Madras — 24
TRUITE AUX AGRUMES
citron bergamote,
& sabayon
noisettes du Piémont &
FOIE GRAS,
viande séchée du Valais, oignons caramélisés
au vinaigre de cidre — 32
FRENCHIE CROQUE COQUIN,
truffe noire — 35
SNACKS
BACON SCONES
crème crue (4 pièces) — 12
GOUGÈRES
sauce mornay au Gruyère & truffe noire
(4 pièces) — 16
ASSIETTE VALAISANNE
lard séché, fromage de Bagnes,
bon cru & pickles — 16/30
séché & oignons — 14
PLATS

LEFT: Charcuterie tastes better when it's served on an antique cutting board. This is a medley of regionally cured meats and raclette cheese from Bagnes, Switzerland, that's served at Frenchie in Verbier.

BELOW: The more you can tailor the little things to your mountain home, the more stylish it will be. I long to walk away with these slippers from the Experimental Chalet Verbier.

ABOVE: "The woodwork paneling was original to the house—we loved its character and warmth," says designer Melinda James of this Virginia home. "The vintage landscape was salvaged from an old farmhouse on the property."

OPPOSITE: Antique beams from a mill in Louisiana that specializes in storied wood help add to the Scottish hunting lodge aesthetic in the dining room. Multiple tables bring more flexibility to the space.

BAILEY
EST. 1864

We custom-ordered this flag on Etsy for our Colorado mountain home; the loose strings are intentional, and help it look as "vintage" as circa 2002 Abercrombie jeans.

UNDERNEATH: Schumacher's sumptuous Woodland Leopard velvet, made in Belgium.

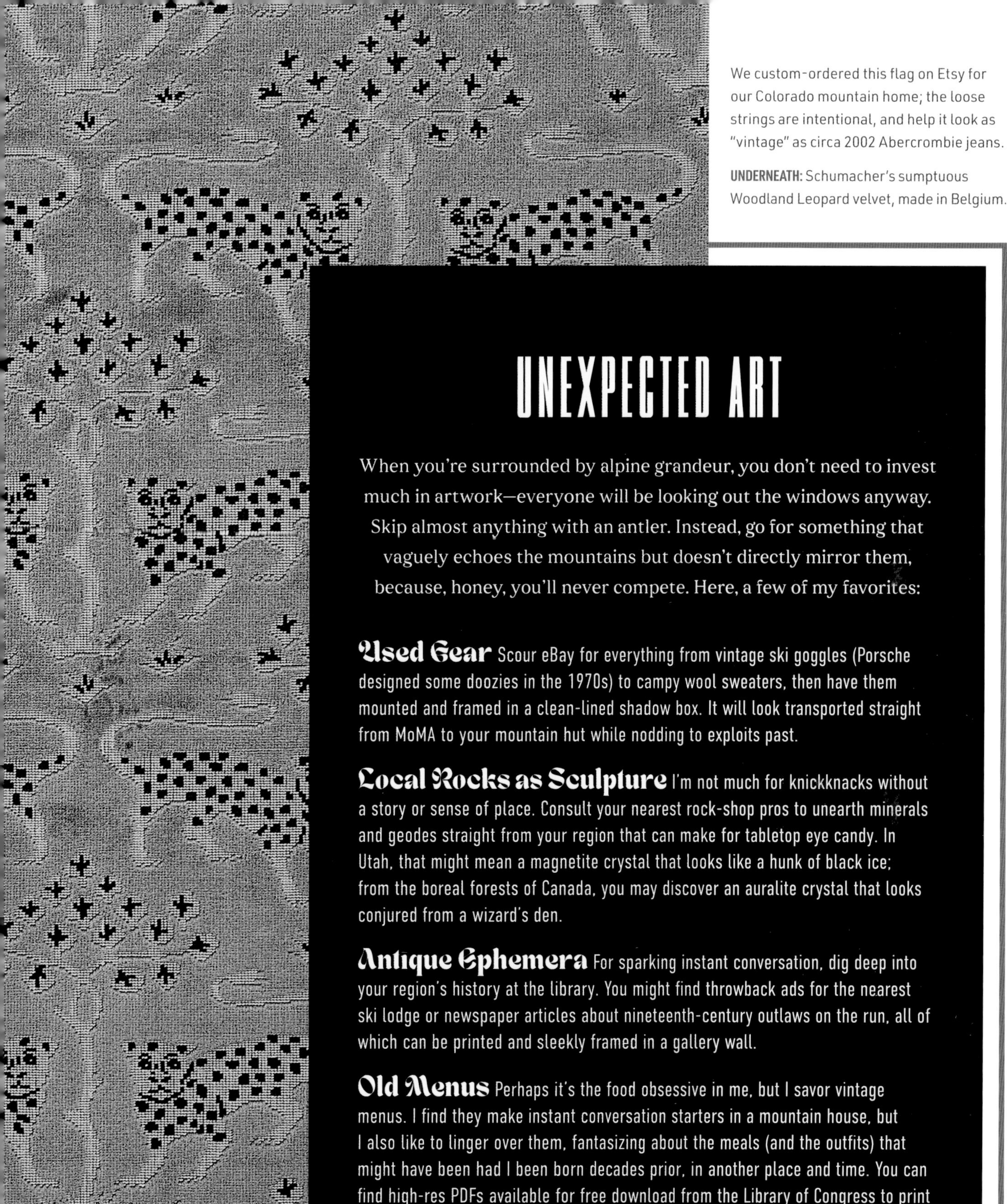

UNEXPECTED ART

When you're surrounded by alpine grandeur, you don't need to invest much in artwork—everyone will be looking out the windows anyway. Skip almost anything with an antler. Instead, go for something that vaguely echoes the mountains but doesn't directly mirror them, because, honey, you'll never compete. Here, a few of my favorites:

Used Gear Scour eBay for everything from vintage ski goggles (Porsche designed some doozies in the 1970s) to campy wool sweaters, then have them mounted and framed in a clean-lined shadow box. It will look transported straight from MoMA to your mountain hut while nodding to exploits past.

Local Rocks as Sculpture I'm not much for knickknacks without a story or sense of place. Consult your nearest rock-shop pros to unearth minerals and geodes straight from your region that can make for tabletop eye candy. In Utah, that might mean a magnetite crystal that looks like a hunk of black ice; from the boreal forests of Canada, you may discover an auralite crystal that looks conjured from a wizard's den.

Antique Ephemera For sparking instant conversation, dig deep into your region's history at the library. You might find throwback ads for the nearest ski lodge or newspaper articles about nineteenth-century outlaws on the run, all of which can be printed and sleekly framed in a gallery wall.

Old Menus Perhaps it's the food obsessive in me, but I savor vintage menus. I find they make instant conversation starters in a mountain house, but I also like to linger over them, fantasizing about the meals (and the outfits) that might have been had I been born decades prior, in another place and time. You can find high-res PDFs available for free download from the Library of Congress to print yourself, or originals on eBay.

OPPOSITE: Made in Scotland by Stark, this rug brought together all the hues of this Todd Richesin-designed home in one preppy plaid. "I chose it because it blended the colors from all over the house," he says. The prints of Scottish clans are from Richesin's antique shop, Bobby Todd.

ABOVE: Paired with tartan draperies, this Tennessee homeowner's collected antler mounts give this Todd Richesin space the air of Scotland's Balmoral Castle, which Queen Victoria deemed "my dear paradise in the Highlands."

OPPOSITE: In Chile, Torres del Paine National Park includes subpolar forests and Patagonian steppes—but it's toothlike granite massifs like these that get all the fanfare.

ABOVE: Designer Kara Adam paired a Gerard Curtis Delano painting with small-scale Phillip Jeffries wallpaper and a timeworn rug in this Crested Butte, Colorado, home. The goal (clearly achieved): "a layered, cozy feel right when you come in off the slopes," Adam says.

ABOVE: This Wyoming home designed by Astrid Sommer Interiors was constructed from four reclaimed two-hundred-year-old cabins from the American South via Kerry Hix, beautifully resuscitated by John K. Walker of Mill Iron Timberworks.

OPPOSITE: Sommer brought in a medley of woven textiles, including vintage Navajo blankets, to warm up the soaring reclaimed beams in the interior. Layering rugs adds to the effect and supplies comfort underfoot.

MARK TWAIN

OPPOSITE: Even a nosegay of blooms, be they prairie roses or anemones, says so much at a guest's bedside table. In short: "Welcome, we're so glad you're here!"

TOP LEFT: Well-loved books—not too many, not too few—styled by Foxtail Books & Library Services, are part of the charm of this Wyoming cabin, which was constructed from centuries-old cabins from the American South.

TOP RIGHT: A cuppa always tastes better by a roaring fire, served in a handmade and hand-painted ceramic mug.

Alternatives to PUMPKIN SPICE LATTES

◆

If you say *pshaw* to a PSL, you may be like me. I like the concept and general autumnal vibe of a pumpkin spice latte but I don't necessarily love the branding that's been quite literally shoved down our throats since the advent of the drink in the early aughts. The seasonal allure of this perking tipple can be had in other similarly creamy, dreamy drinks, especially when you add steamed milk and a dusting of nutmeg, cinnamon, or clove. Try these come early September, when that first crisp morning hits.

Chai Latte In India, chai (black tea) has been sipped for thousands of years, often mixed into a masala chai with sugar, milk, and a heady blend of regional spices from ginger to cardamom. Would you expect anything less than cozy in the home of the Himalayas?

London Fog Among the most popular cuppa in Britain since the 1830s, Earl Grey tea got its name when Charles Grey—the second Earl Grey—served as prime minister. Flavored with citrusy bergamot oil, the tea becomes even more heavenly when mixed with steamed milk and vanilla or even lavender syrup, when it becomes a poetically named London Fog.

Caramel Apple Cider Apples have been a beloved part of the fall season since they were first cultivated in what's now Kazakhstan. Medieval monks of Europe perfected the art of pressing them into cider, and in the US colonies, apple cider was often slurped more than water, which was frequently thought too impure to drink. I love mixing a bit of caramel into my apple cider; on snow days, I keep the cider itself in the slow cooker so it's at the ready when we come in from playing in the powder, a move that has the added benefit of making the whole house smell incredible.

OPPOSITE: Basalt, Colorado-based designer Kam Davies brought a European feel to this outdoor table in Aspen, with its Belgian linen tablecloth, U.K.-handmade plates, and custom handblown indigo candle sticks designed by Davies. The hues echo the topography, and the comfortable setup encourages guests "to laugh and linger," Davies says.

ABOVE: This Aspen bar designed by Davies lures après-ski and après-fishing guests. "The creamy, brown leathered countertop is a rugged, beautiful complement to the Farrow & Ball Studio Green cabinets," Davies says. The pottery bowl was commissioned from a local artist; the painting of Colorado aspens brings in the surrounding flora.

Adapted from the J-Bar at the Hotel Jerome, Auberge Resorts Collection, Aspen, Colorado

ASPEN CRUD

I call this delightful shake "Prohibition punch" because it was born at the height of the Prohibition era. Aspen regulars know it as the "Aspen Crud" because it has been served at the 1889 Hotel Jerome's J-Bar (a favorite watering hole of the journalist Hunter S. Thompson) since circa 1920. That's when the longtime pub was transformed into a "soda fountain," and asking for a "crud" would get you a milkshake with a wink of bourbon. It's iconic for a good reason.

YIELD: 1 SERVING

4 ounces whole milk

2 ounces bourbon (I like Boulder Spirits Bourbon)

3 large scoops vanilla ice cream

Whipped cream

Blend all ingredients (except the whipped cream) until it's the consistency of a throwback milkshake: velvety and thick. Serve in a chilled tumbler, and top with an avalanche of whipped cream.

I like to sneak down to the Hotel Jerome's lobby at dawn, when there's nobody there. It's one of my favorite spaces in Colorado—best soaked up in blissful silence.

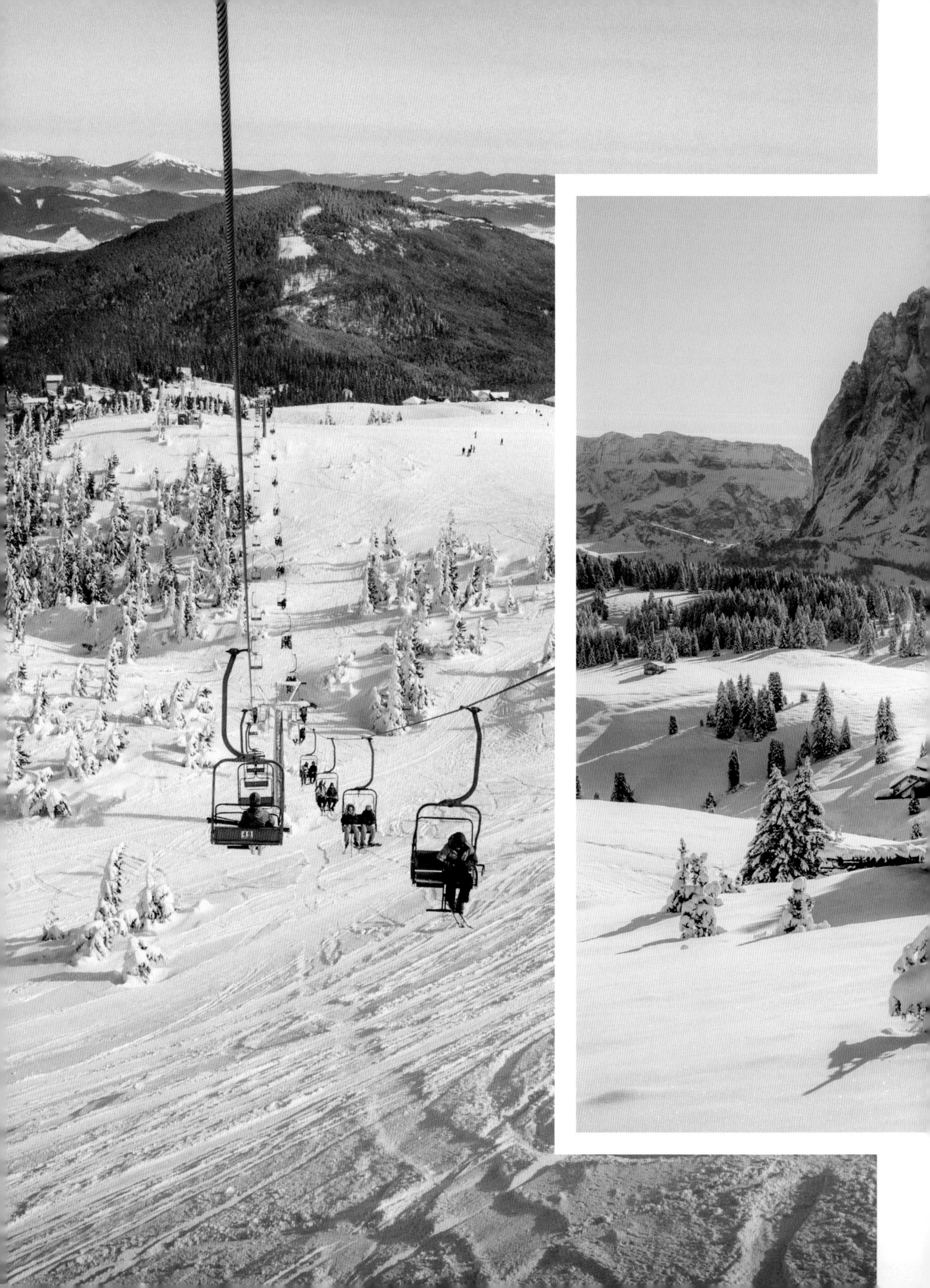

Winter

Lech Zürs am Arlberg, a ski resort in Austria, always beckoned to Princess Diana at first flake. She brought her boys there often; they'd check into the Hotel Arlberg Lech and check out what it was like to be footloose and fancy-free, for once—well, as footloose as one can be on skis.

On the slopes, a celeb isn't a celeb. Wrapped up like mummies in ski gear (and hopefully helmets), they're as unrecognizable as anybunny else. They can shush and slalom with the unfettered glee of an alpine chamois, then zip to the chalet for a cocktail. And if that chalet is stocked with a flickering fire and a hot tub overlooking the craggy peaks? That's a recipe for what Dolly Parton would call "springtime feelings in the middle of December"—a.k.a. heat, at any temperature.

When snow is swirling and wind is howling, you want to do as a marmot does: burrow and nest with the best. Top your beds with eiderdown bed toppers; trot out rich velvet pillows and cashmere blankets with a playful fringe for texture; and toss thick faux or vintage hides and furry pelts over chairbacks, indoors and out. Make sure each and every rug you have is set over a beefy rug pad, which at its best adds plump sumptuousness underfoot and at a minimum helps prevent slipping. Put something charming on the stereo to lighten the stark, gray sky-mood. (Vince Guaraldi's 1964 "Linus and Lucy" is a favorite in our house.)

ABOVE: The family-run Forsthofgut hotel in Leogang, Austria, sits on a circa 1617 forestry farm. Architecture marries the regional vernacular with a slick modernity that suits its sprawling spa.

OPPOSITE: Forsthofgut is slopeside amid the 70 ski lifts at Saalbach-Hinterglemm-Leogang-Fieberbrunn, which means you're approximately three minutes from the steam baths when you get off a run.

PREVIOUS: Diana, Princess of Wales, in the Swiss ski resort of Klosters in February 1987.

ABOVE: The regional, seasonal dishes at Forsthofgut have included asparagus from Marchfeld, Austria, served with a swirl of hollandaise, potatoes, and prosciutto from Heidewuggerl farm in Burgenland.

RIGHT: A resident family at Forsthofgut.

FOLLOWING PAGE: The modernism of the Lake House at Forsthofgut obtrudes beautifully amid the Leogang Rocky Mountains.

. . . so many of us turn inward that they call December 21 the

HIBERNAL

Solstice.

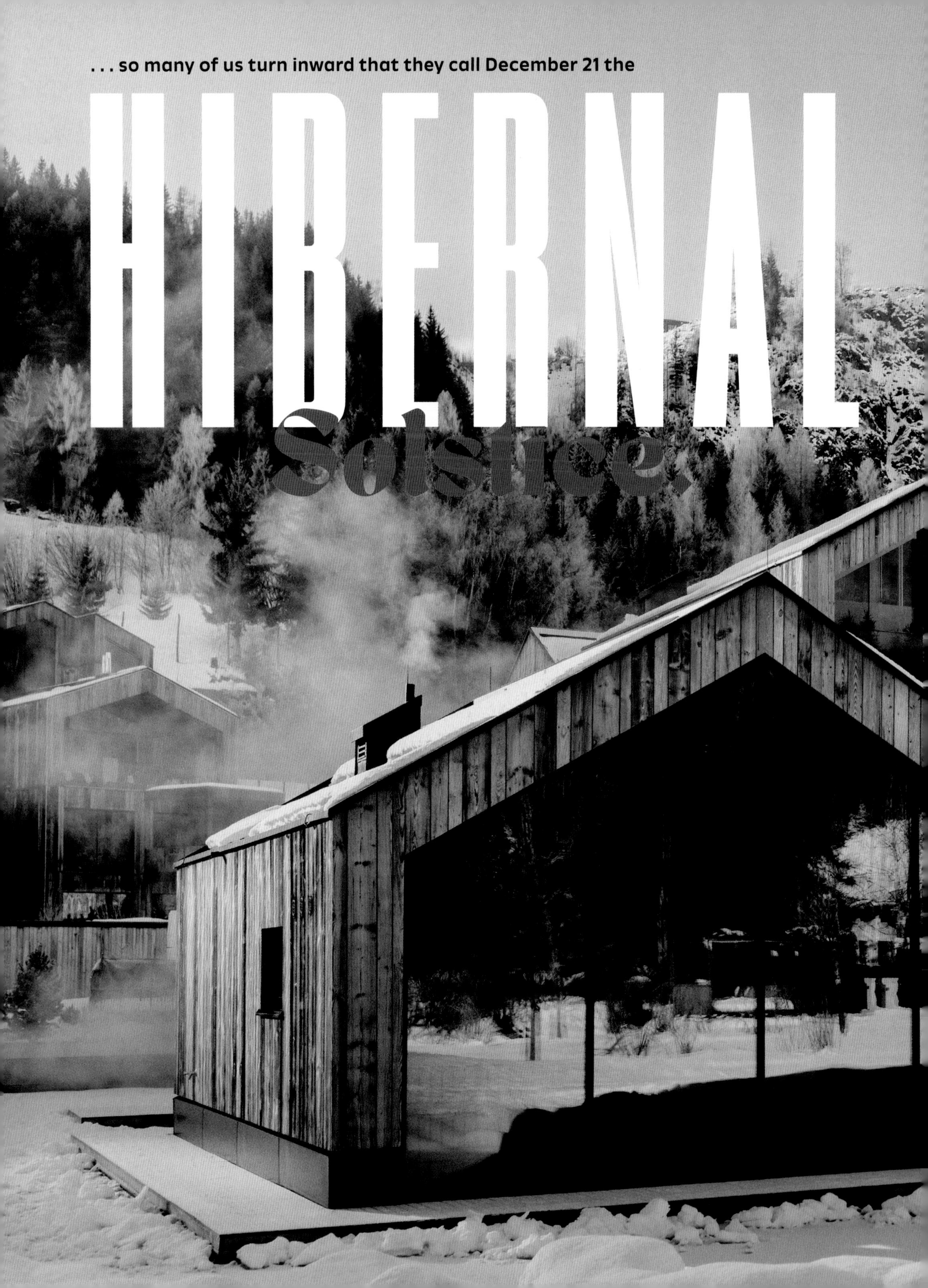

Clearly, warmth is crucial in winter—and cranking up the thermostat can only do so much. Swapping your cooler LED light bulbs for ones with a higher color temperature (2700k–3000k) can almost—*almost*—recreate the appeal of recently extradited incandescents. Candles, too. We don't use actual open flames at our mountain house because we don't want to tempt the forest-fire gods (Can you imagine being *that* neighbor?), but humanity has achieved practical magic with battery-powered varieties. Squint and you can practically see flames dance.

OPPOSITE: My husband and I loved the black exteriors we noticed in Iceland; they've used tar for generations to protect timber from frequent blizzards. This Búðir church, shot by Robert Peterson and available on Artfully Walls, sits in the Búðahraun lava field.

THE FACT IS,

LIFE HAPPENS,

especially in the mountains.

I'm a Christmas obsessive, but even if I were agnostic, I think I'd see the appeal of bringing twinkly lights and evergreen cuttings indoors late November through February. It's dreary and grave in winter, and so many of us turn inward that they call December 21 the "hibernal solstice." Without an escape hatch to a tropical sojourn, a freshly harvested sprig of cypress or Scotch pine can be a fragrant salve, an olfactory promise that warmer days are coming.

And you don't want everything in your house to look too perfect. (This is something we easily achieve in our primary house in suburban Denver, which often looks like a nor'easter has just blown through!) The fact is, life happens, especially in the mountains. The leather should get a bit scuffed; the fur nubby and matted. The same way people can mistrust a rail-thin chef, no one will ever feel quite comfortable in a mountain house that looks like it was trucked in yesterday from a furniture showroom in the city. Ride it hard, like a pair of Rossignol. ◆

OPPOSITE: A log-inspired table brings the outdoors into this gondola-front seating area in Stowe, Vermont, designed by Michelle Holland of Nantucket House. Binoculars are always a nice touch in a mountain house: all the better to spot black-capped chickadees and loved ones schussing down the slopes.

ABOVE: Skiing the Dolomites (shown here: a lift connected to Forestis, a modernist hotel in the South Tyrolean portion of Italy), is such a bona fide bucket-list experience it has credentials: the range was named a UNESCO World Heritage Site in 2009.

FOLLOWING PAGE: The 2,152-square foot penthouse at Forestis in Italy—designed by Asaggio, a Brixen-based architecture firm—where your private terrace has a pool and spruce wood sauna overlooking the Dolomites.

A freshly harvested

SPRIG OF CYPRESS

or

SCOTCH PINE

can be a fragrant salve, an olfactory promise that warmer days are coming.

DAY AFTER

UPON THE

GROWING

FROM END

SUNSHINE

THE LIGHT, CLEAR AND D

LIKE CRYSTAL.

The bathhouse at Dunton Hot Springs on the outskirts of Telluride, Colorado. (Not shown, because it's hidden behind a tree: an outdoor hot spring that's ideal for steeping in newly fallen snow.)

WINTER CHALET TOUR
The Berkshires, Massachusetts

◆

Fun is not a frequently used descriptor in the architectural world, where verbiage leans more toward words like *massing* and *materiality*. But this home peering out on Massachusetts's Mount Greylock, designed by the New York firm Workshop/APD, is unequivocally *fun*. Orange ski-lift chair in the mudroom? Check. Bunks high as the sky? Check and check. It's got all the merriment of a snow day, brought indoors from the cold.

ABOVE: In this mudroom in the Berkshires, Workshop/APD installed a refurbished tangerine orange ski lift from Colorado-based Ski Lift Designs.

RIGHT: Under a nearly sixteen-foot ceiling peak, a three-level oak sleeping space by Workshop/APD has bunks for six—plus storage drawers tucked below the bottom beds (note drawer pulls).

OPPOSITE: Skis as decor can sometimes feel theme-y. But placed in an X along a long hallway by Workshop/APD, these are graphic and almost sculptural.

The exposed beams and window placement in this primary bedroom designed by Workshop/APD remind me of a ryokan in Japan in their serene simplicity. The duo of ottomans are Tibetan lamb fur.

OPPOSITE: On our last trip to Aspen, I made my husband pull over so I could dash out of the car to take this photo of the 1969 interfaith Aspen Chapel under a fresh dusting of snow.

ABOVE: Freezing flowers in a block of ice creates a show-stopping bar for parties. The upland white aster grows from Quebec to Colorado.

It doesn't seem so much

TO CLIMB A MOUNTAIN

You've worked around the foot of all your life.

—ROBERT FROST, "THE MOUNTAIN," 1914

OPPOSITE: A sunny slopeside perch at Pitztaler Gletscher & Rifflsee ski resort in Austria. Note the powder-blue interior color of the lower shutters, a perfect match for the sky.

OPPOSITE: A trio of stone-topped coffee tables—the same height of the seats, a must for comfort—ensure everyone has a place to rest their drink.

ABOVE: In a Montana ski chalet designed by Seattle-based Kylee Shintaffer and Bozeman's Miller Roodell Architects, the proverbial power desk has a power view: the snow-dusted Rocky Mountains. The chair is vintage, by Paul McCobb.

LEFT: Look closely at the canopy bed Shintaffer placed at left, and you'll notice iron birds alighting on the upper rail. The built-in bunks are perfect for corralling the family for strictly enforced "we time."

ABOVE: Melinda James hung an unexpected light fixture in this Virginia library: designed by Nickey Kehoe for Urban Electric, in a custom finished metal, it was inspired by seventeenth-century Bibliothèque Mazarine in Paris.

OPPOSITE: Pressed botanicals from Belgium anchor the wall behind this circa 1860 plank-board table, which James sourced from the Veuve Pommery Champagne house near Reims, France. Two layers of Schumacher fabrics—the Hugo Floral in jute and linen and Stella, small-scale stars—add a beautiful layered effect.

PICKING A SUMPTUOUS FAUX-FUR BLANKET

What to Look For

◆

I love a natural fiber blanket—a wool *cashmericle,* especially—as much as the next girl, but sometimes only a fluffy faux-fur blanket will do. That's especially true in the glacial days of winter. It's primal. Our earliest ancestors donned the pelts of golden jackals, sand foxes, and wildcats, after all. So if I want to cache myself away under a puddle of fur meant to mimic a Kodiak bear, that's my prerogative!

Unfortunately, not all faux furs are created equal. The worst offenders smell like plastic and look a bit like an arcade-prize teddy bear that's been reincarnated to scratch, matt, and shed hairs at every turn. Here's how to avoid that:

Splurge With anything tactile, you get what you pay for. If you want a faux-fur blanket that will last years and look like the real thing, it's worth investing in it. We spent several hundred dollars on the RH faux-fur blanket that we toss over the back of the game-room sofa at our vacation rental, Skytop Mountain House, and it still looks brand new.

Go Ombre As far as coiffures go, the animals of the world's mountains look like they've hit the salon for a balayage. The fur of the Tibetan sand fox slips from a tangerine to a gunmetal gray; a chamois is tan, chestnut, and umber all at once. Most iconic of all may be the Himalayan tahr, which appears to wear a lion's mane around its auburn body—fresh from a blowout. To that end, you never want to buy a fur blanket that is one-note in its color. It will look flat, dull, and dreary.

Maintenance Muddy boots happen. Ditto spills of syrah. And when they do, you'll be happier if you selected a well-made, quality faux fur that can be cleaned without disintegrating. Dry-clean only is a good sign of a quality purchase and worth every red dime.

ABOVE: Rather than break up this Montana living space into a myriad of disjointed seating arrangements, designer Kylee Shintaffer employed two custom sixteen-foot-long, wool-upholstered sectionals that everyone can pile into for après-ski. The bleached stump tables from Sawkille Co. bring nature in.

OPPOSITE: Even the most utilitarian spaces in the world can and should be beautiful, as this ski storage mudroom designed by Shintaffer attests. The screen on the cabinet doors hides away gear a bit for a more serene look.

JUNGFRAUJOCH
JUNGFRAUBAHN

Astrid Sommer Interiors brought antique Navajo textiles aplenty into this Wyoming cabin. Underleaf fabric at right: Schumacher's handmade Samarkand Ikat II, in cotton.

RIGHT: A well-lit corner practically begs for a reading table. You can see the ax marks on the exposed beams here—antique cabins transported to Wyoming for this home designed by Astrid Sommer Interiors.

OPPOSITE: Held back by fallen antlers, these thick portières that enclose the foyer add softness and serve to preserve heat when closed. The stone floor in the entrance is a prescient touch—perfect for shaking off your boots before entry.

FOLLOWING PAGE: A rolling market basket is a forever stylish hideaway for walking sticks, especially juxtaposed beneath a gilt twig mirror and audubon ceiling wallpaper in this Virginia pass-through designed by Melinda James.

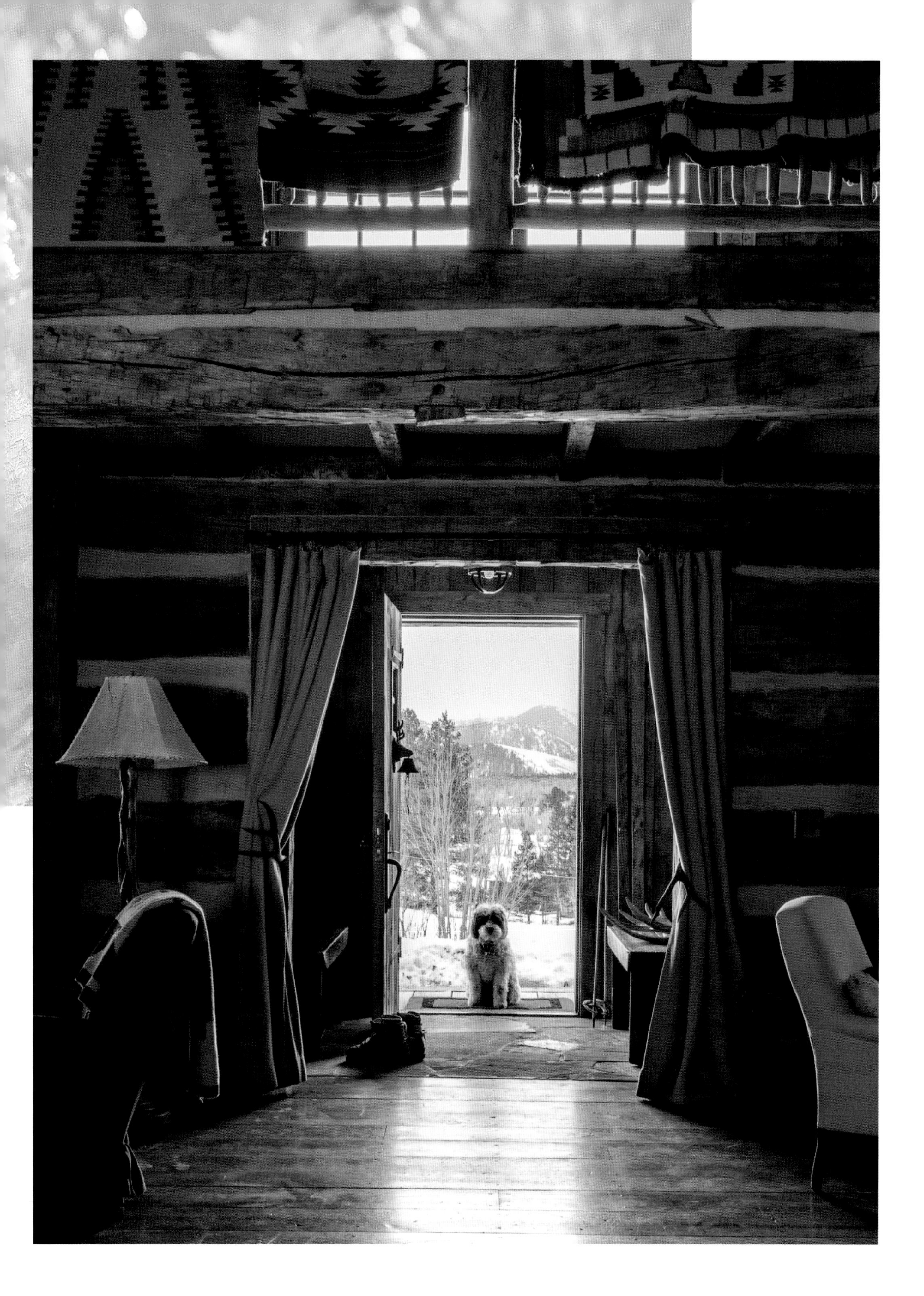

Thousands of tired, nerve-shaken, over-civilized people are beginning to find out that going to the mountains is going home; that wildness is a necessity; and that mountain parks and reservations are useful not only as fountains of timber and irrigating rivers, but as fountains of life.

–JOHN MUIR, *OUR NATIONAL PARKS*, 1901

Upgrade Your Fire

◆

It's vital to use local firewood as often as you can, to avoid giving parasitic pests (like Rocky Mountain pine beetles) a free ride to their next victim forest. So while I might prefer using hickory or cherry wood logs for their scent, here in Colorado I often have to opt for what's readily available in the region.

You can fancify your fire by adding fragrance in other ways, such as tossing in a small bundle of dried sage or rosemary; cinnamon sticks and cloves; or lavender. Dried leftover citrus peels—like slivers of orange, lemon, or even grapefruit—can give a tidy blaze a bit of a tropical edge. Just remember to keep fire safety protocols in mind—a fire is a fire.

Adapted from the Chesa al Parc Restaurant at Kulm Hotel, St. Moritz, Switzerland

CHEESE FONDUE

Given its DIY element, fondue—the beloved Swiss dish of melted cheese, wine, and garlic that got its name from the French word *fondre*, "to melt"—could well be called fun-do. This particular recipe comes from the circa 1856 Kulm Hotel in St. Moritz, Switzerland, where it's best enjoyed on the terrace overlooking the slopes. Dip whatever you like into it; I go for bread and more bread.

YIELD: 2 SERVINGS

1 garlic clove, sliced in half
6 ounces mild Nufenen cheese
6 ounces strong Nufenen cheese
5 ounces Vacherin Fribourgeois
¾ cup dry white wine
3 teaspoons potato starch
4 teaspoons cherry brandy

Rub the inside of the *caquelon* (fondue pot) with sliced garlic clove. Grate all cheeses and place them in the pot. Add white wine and mix. In a separate bowl, mix the potato starch with cherry brandy and add to the *caquelon*. Place on medium heat and stir until the fondue is creamy.

***If you can't find Nufenen cheese, Gruyère, raclette, or Emmentaler are good substitutes.**

Spring

Something glorious happens after the thaw, and it's not yet another round of viral videos of grizzly bears emerging from hibernation, much in need of a hairbrush (although, if you haven't watched one, do so immediately!). No, what I'm referring to is so vital it is in all of us. Actually, it *is* us. All of us. Water.

That's right—each spring, the waterfalls barreling over craggy cliffs go from their iced wintry trickle to a downright deluge. Snow melts into the earth, refilling the coffers of mountain wells like our own version of Pellegrino, bottled at the source in the Dolomites. And—my favorite—the winter-weary grasses go from a parched, rutty brown to emerald green seemingly overnight, a viridescent cure for my British-Irish bones.

BELOW: There are approximately eighty-two thousand wild horses roaming the American West, and they're all descended from the domesticated ones brought here in the sixteenth century that then become feral and untamed.

PREVIOUS: Melinda James swapped the existing walls in this Virginia home for bronze windows and doors they designed "to maximize the views down to the riding paddocks and the Shenandoah mountains beyond," James says.

HOTEL

In a Sun Valley, Idaho, retreat, Jennifer Miller Studio whipped up a nook overlooking the pines, and transformed vintage Navajo rugs into accent pillows.

OPPOSITE: Large-scale photographs of owls by Leila Jeffreys are a hoot in the open dining room designed by Jennifer Miller, where plaster and a reclaimed-beam ceiling play off one another. The custom bench on one side of the table brings a coziness that wouldn't be there if all the seats were matchy-matchy.

ABOVE: Miller employed a Soane fabric on the Roman shades in this guest suite, where plaster walls and sloped wood ceilings add to the chalet feel.

Heavy blankets and stocky pillows are consigned to storage, and out come happy accessories with all the charm of a calypso orchid: gauzy linen draperies, botanical tableware, sky-blue glassware. Because I hate to cull the fresh bumper crop of wildflowers out the windows, I like to put together a transfixing bowl of moss for the living-room table, the shade of emerald wellies. After months in a world awash in shades of brown and white, I crave bracing greens the same way I crave water after a hike. I'm parched and listless when I go too long or too far without it.

I also like to take this season as my cue to do a bit of spring cleaning and organizing, a tradition cultures across the globe have embraced for centuries in the season of rebirth, and still do today.

OPPOSITE: The lead cladding on this soaking tub in a Tom Riker–designed home near Deer Lodge, Montana, lends it a note of rusticity that echoes the surrounding peaks. Laying the marble floor tiles in a herringbone pattern has a timeless effect.

ABOVE: Schumacher's Florentine cut velvet, designed in collaboration with Timothy Corrigan and made in Belgium.

They call it *khāne-takānī* in Iran (or "shaking down the house") and *kathari deftera* (clean Monday) in Greece. Whatever you call it, the concept is the same: get your you-know-what together, and fast. I am not a natural Martha and find I have to arrange a carrot of sorts to reward myself with once the obnoxious task at hand is done. Empty every single drawer and shelf in the kitchen and give all the inner surfaces a good scrubbing? *Boom*—new hiking boots, ordered. Go through our vinyl records and book collection to purge and collate? *Boom*—dinner out at our favorite local winery, reserved.

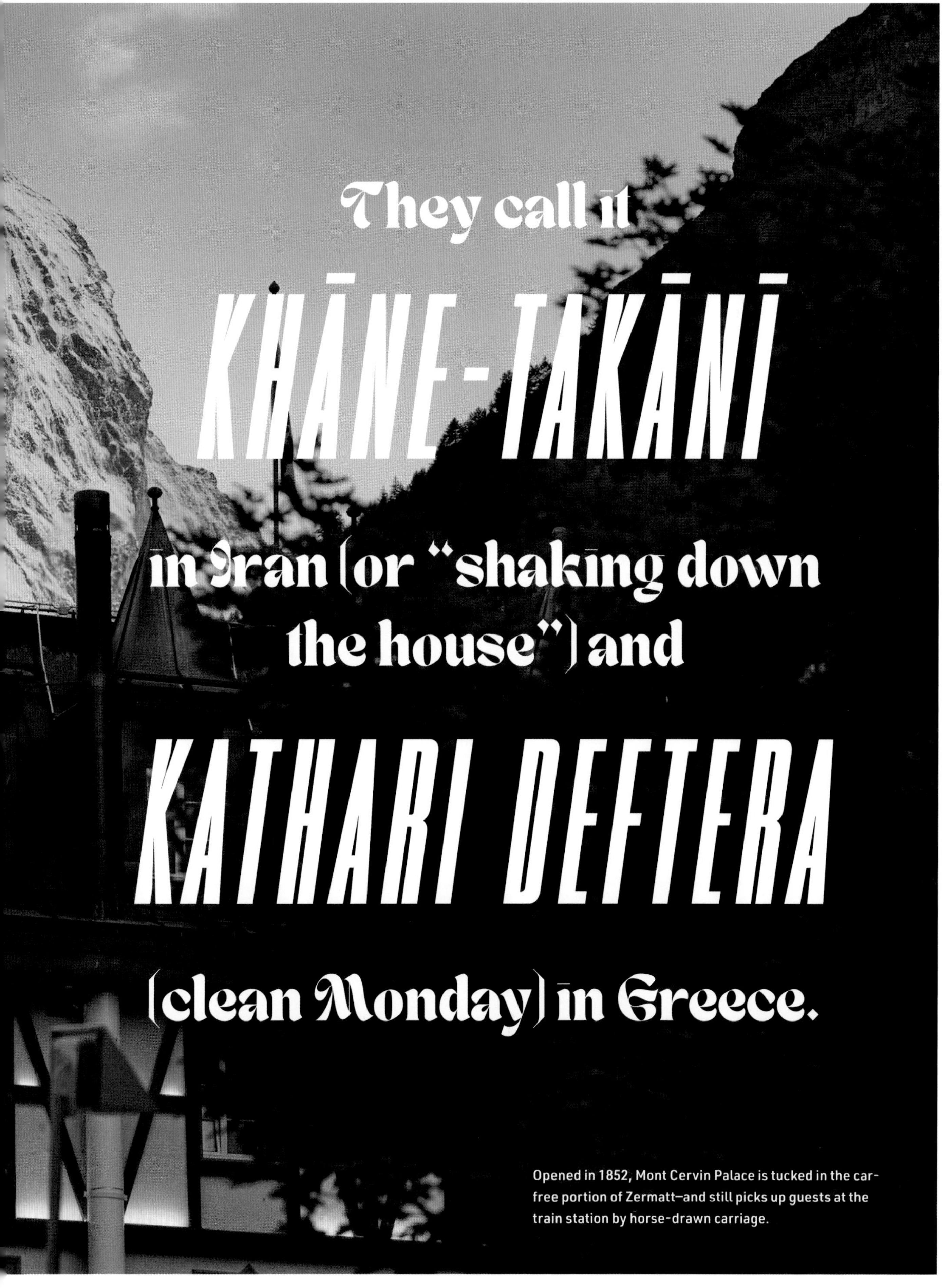

They call it

KHĀNE-TAKĀNĪ

in Iran (or "shaking down the house") and

KATHARI DEFTERA

(clean Monday) in Greece.

Opened in 1852, Mont Cervin Palace is tucked in the car-free portion of Zermatt—and still picks up guests at the train station by horse-drawn carriage.

ABOVE: A switchback floating staircase made of white oak and dark steel allows daylight to flow into this Berkshires home designed by Workshop/APD untrammeled.

OPPOSITE: Accordion windows can fold open on early spring's rare yet delightful balmy days. The stump table was the client's own, and placed next to a swing chair by Workshop/APD.

POWDER
ICE IS
LAURENT
CHASING EPIC

ABOVE LEFT: In Deer Valley, Utah, the firm Massucco Warner brought the wilderness indoors in a classical way with a parade of framed waterfowl and fallen horn transformed into sculpture.

ABOVE RIGHT: A bench with a narrow footprint is just enough of a perch to lug on snow boots while letting the vintage kilim rug take center stage in this Utah foyer by the design firm Massucco Warner.

OPPOSITE: Painting the existing exposed timber and trusses a deep gray helped them recede a bit, preventing this Deer Valley, Utah, living space by Massucco Warner from reading too mountain theme-y.

We keep things in our mountain house minimal, but still there are things to check off the list each spring. Some we can do ourselves—like replacing all our bed and bath linens with new pristine white ones. Other chores we hire the pros to do, like having professional window cleaners come to wash our many windows clear or—a humdrum reality of mountain life—having our well water tested for purity and enlisting the septic gurus to do whatever they do. Either way, 'tis the season to start over. You'll feel as refreshed and new as the delicate pasque flowers pushing purply through the earth.

RALPH LAUREN

FRIULI FOOD AND WINE

OPPOSITE: The walls of the Blackberry Farm cottage are sheathed in hickory, native to the region. Designer Tammy Connor employed natural textures (wool draperies, supple leather, wood galore) in the living space; the result feels familiar and not overly formal.

ABOVE: Connor brought the verdant spring greens of Tennessee's Smoky Mountains into this guest-cottage kitchen by painting the cabinets Benjamin Moore's Shady Lane in a hard-wearing semigloss finish.

THE FRESH BUMPER CROP OF

wildflowers out the windows

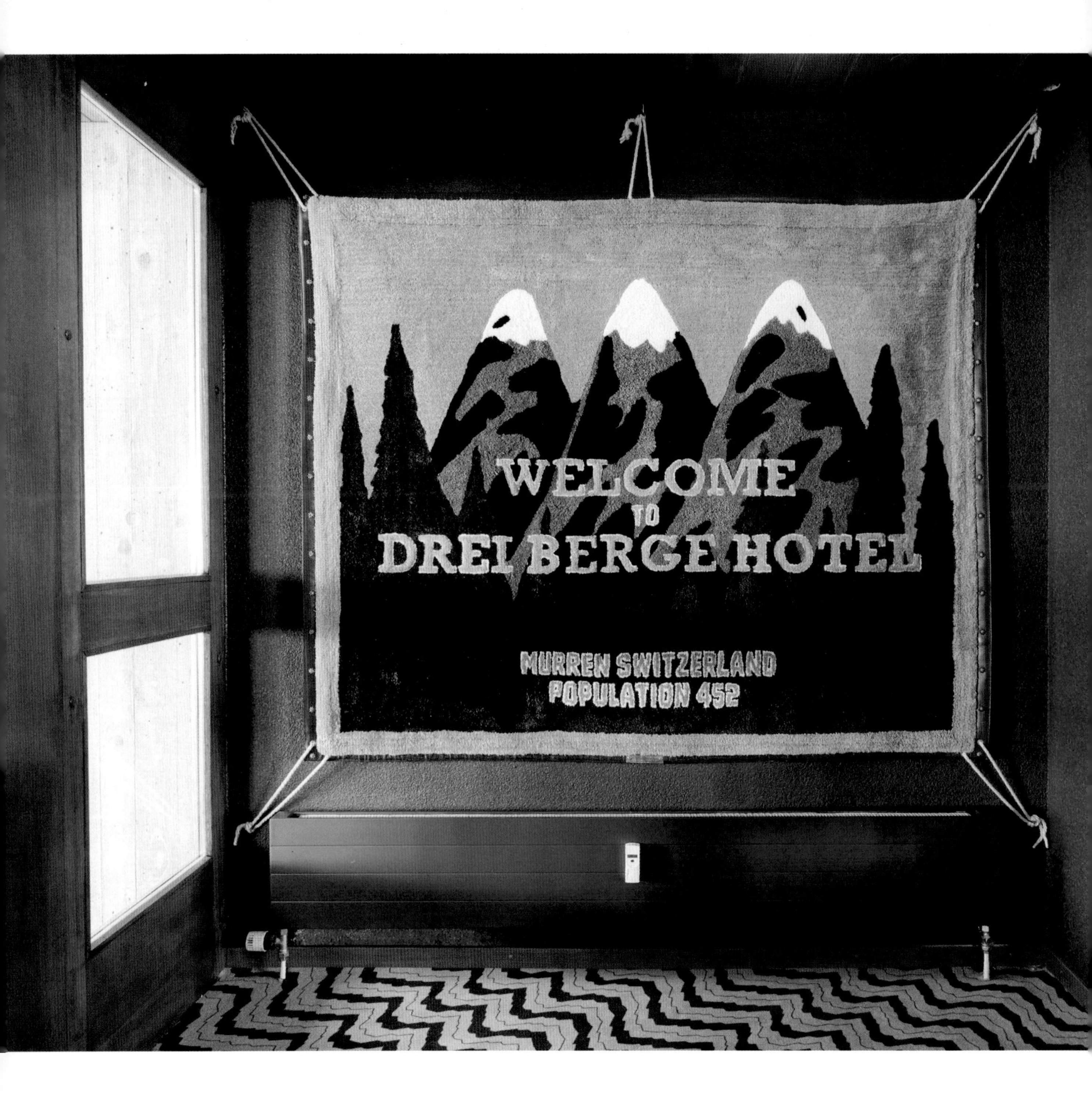

ABOVE: Paris-based creative director and artist Ramdane Touhami is the hotelier behind Drei Berge Hotel in Mürren, Switzerland. This custom piece at the entry is "a reminder carpet . . . these are the mountains I've climbed and the ones I want to climb," Touhami says.

OPPOSITE: Touhami painted the exterior shutters of the circa 1907 structure red and white. "I spotted a building with shutters like this on the route de Berne in Mürren, and thought it would be a nice idea," Touhami recalls.

FOLLOWING PAGE: Touhami and his team kept much of the hotel's original woodwork and added more of their own chevron details and crown moldings. "The coats of arms represent the great Swiss families," Touhami says. "I came across a book from the sixteenth century with the Swiss coats of arms."

DREI BERGE HOTEL
SEIT 1907

Cabin Fever

Drei Berge Hotel

YOU'LL FEEL AS REFRESHED AND NEW
as the delicate
pasque flowers
pushing purply
through
the earth.

OPPOSITE: The custom rugs at Drei Berge Hotel in Mürren, Switzerland, designed by Ramdane Touhami.

ABOVE: "The pennants are again those mountains I want to climb," says Touhami, who designed them in his own Paris studio. Note the mounts and vintage skis studding the ceiling.

ABOVE: Every detail is thought of at Touhami's Drei Berge, down to the keychains for the nineteen guest rooms and custom-designed beds and monogrammed linens. Touhami's creative agency, Art Recherche Industrie, masterminds it all.

OPPOSITE: Exterior hues at Drei Berge are, authentically, a bit muddy—which brings them in line with the surrounding landscape.

ERGE
HOTEL
SEIT 1907
RESTAURANT
KAFFEE
MÜRREN
Julius Meinl
Berger
Tell
Drei Berge Hotel
WHITE HORSE
SWITZERLAND
HOTEL OPEN ALL YEAR

The greens used in the thirty-nine-room Experimental Chalet in Verbier, designed by Fabrizio Casiraghi, are close matches to the forest palettes on the adjacent slopes—where trees like Norway spruce, European silver firs, and Swiss pine proliferate.

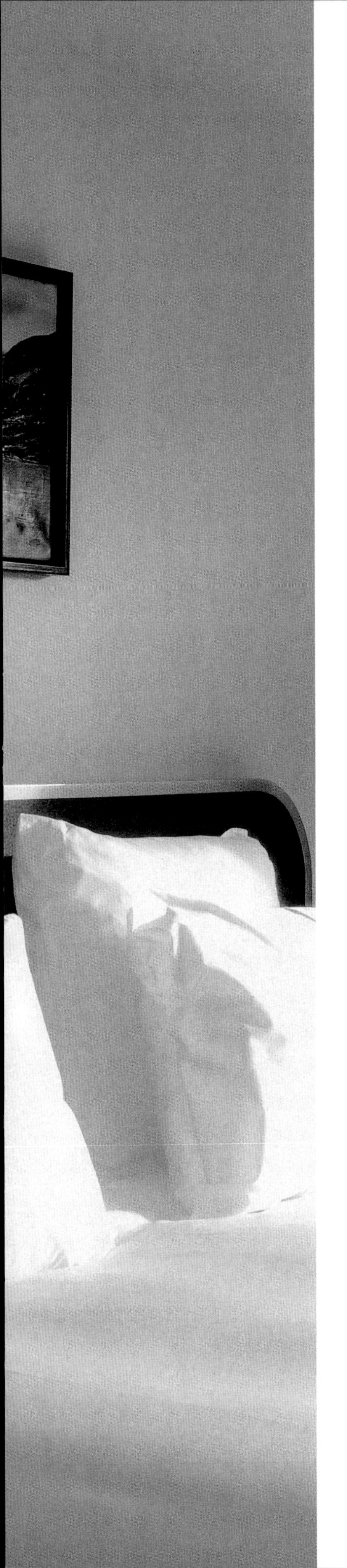

WHAT'S IN A NAME?
Everything, Darling

◆

I've always believed that country houses should have names—something more poetic and evocative than just their destination or address, which is the equivalent of naming a child Bob (not that there's anything wrong with that). These houses are like members of the family, after all, and home to some of our most transcendent memories. What would Asheville, North Carolina's Biltmore be if the Vanderbilt's simply called it by its address, "1 Lodge Street?" Sure, the casa in question would still preside over eight thousand acres in the Blue Ridge Mountains . . . but even its French Renaissance–style architecture wouldn't have the same riveting draw.

When my husband and I first purchased the Colorado getaway we run as a short-term rental when we're not using it, we planned on naming it after a nearby street. But that never felt quite right. The structure sits at nearly ten thousand feet in elevation, so soaring you can feel like you're amid the clouds themselves. Eventually it came to us: Skytop Mountain House. Skytop suits, because when we're up there, we feel like we're on top of the world.

To suss out your own moniker for your mountain roost, you may want to look to the following for inspiration:

Local Flora and Fauna On Mexico's eighteen-thousand-foot-high Pico de Orizaba, you might frequently spot the resident cardinal-red warblers . . . and name your *cabina* Warbler's Roost. In the shadows of Alaska's Mount Denali, feltleaf willow is everywhere—which could engender the name Willow's Watch.

The Five Senses Amble out your door and take a deep breath. Are you catching a whiff of ponderosa pine? Piney Point might be a fitting epithet. Do you find the wind especially blustery by your perch? Zephyr's End could be a nomenclature for the ages.

Extracurriculars If yours is a skiing hideout, play with something that instantly says "ski bunnies live here": The Black Diamond, or Slope Shack. Does hiking have your heart? The Pinnacle is a fine honorific.

FARM·CLUB
DISCOTHEQUE
FARM·CLUB
DISCOTHEQUE
FARM·CLUB
DISCOTHEQUE
FARM·CLUB
VERBIER
FARM·CLUB
VERBIER

OPPOSITE: Casiraghi injected classic style into the existing 1950s facade of the Experimental Chalet with candy-apple-red shutters and umbrellas–an exact match to the Swiss flag (adopted in 1841 and as chic as ever).

ABOVE: A two-minute schlep from Schwarzsee cable car station, the Zermatt sign proves you've made it.

SPRING CHALET TOUR
Jackson, Wyoming

◆

Some houses have stories to tell, if you're willing to listen. When the designer Emily Janak began renovations on her family's decidedly "meh" ranch in Jackson, she and her team (including her husband, the architect Adam Janak, partner at Northworks Architects) discovered it had a delightful skeleton in the cupboard: a 1936 pine log cabin tucked away under a thick layer of 1960s drywall. They saved each hulking piece of timber, then erected a family abode that combines the airiness that modern life demands with the original fable-worthy structure.

ABOVE: Cross-corner frames like those leaning against the original logs at this writing desk in Emily and Adam Janak's former home are a mountain mainstay: historic in feel, yet so graphic. The pen-and-ink piece is by Emily's great-grandfather, an engraver who designed the Hallmark logo.

ABOVE: The Janaks linked the original 1936 cabin (right) and its modern wing by staining the exterior a cohesive black: ABR Natural Seal Wood Protective Coating in Weathered Creosote.

OPPOSITE: Hidden underneath the 1960s ranch home, the Janaks found the original 1936 pine logs in pristine condition—a perfect juxtaposition for a modern Nordic kitchen. Dutch doors keep dogs and kids in while allowing fresh mountain air to flow. The fabric under the photo is Schumacher's Florentine Chevron Velvet.

LIVING IN THE MOUNTAINS
THE LOG CABIN
THE HUNTING BOOK
OLIVER DORN

OPPOSITE: A Billy Schenck serigraph, "Gone with the Gunsmoke," brought in an extra dose of Wild West cool to the Janak's living room.

ABOVE: An on-theme but not cliché door knocker is such a lovely touch point; the Janaks selected this trout from Adams & Mack, sand cast in Devon, England.

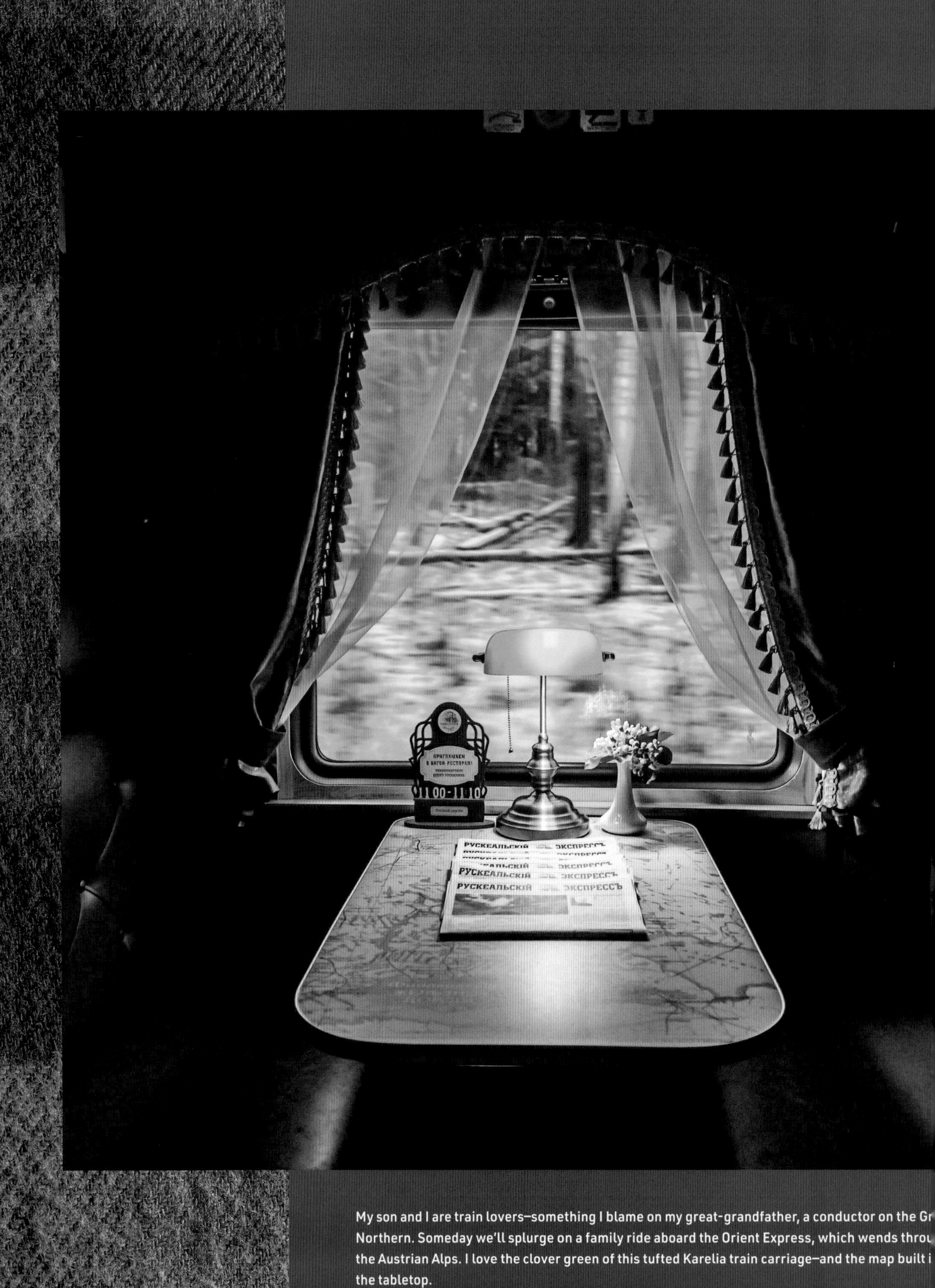

My son and I are train lovers—something I blame on my great-grandfather, a conductor on the Gr
Northern. Someday we'll splurge on a family ride aboard the Orient Express, which wends throu
the Austrian Alps. I love the clover green of this tufted Karelia train carriage—and the map built i
the tabletop.

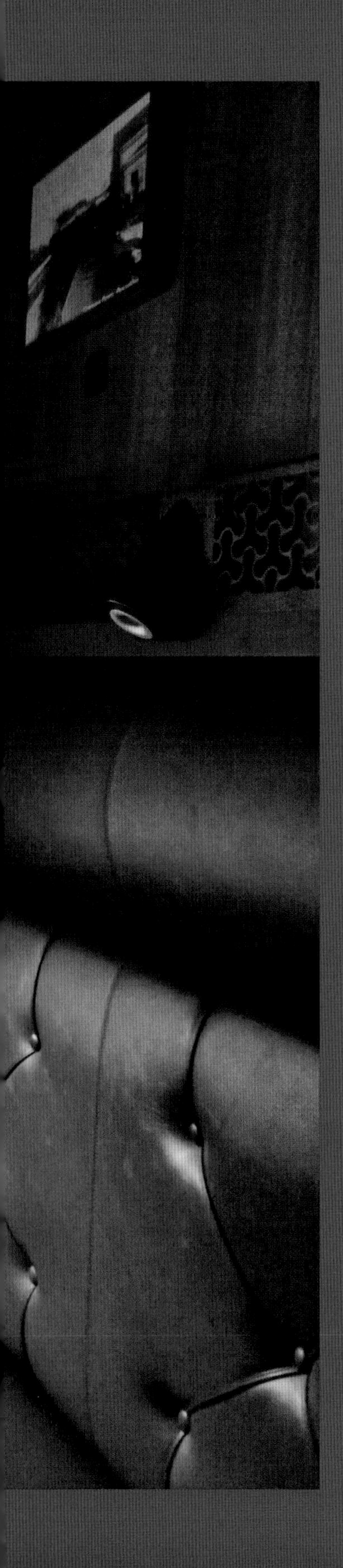

Whoever has made a voyage up the Hudson must remember the Katskill mountains.

They are a dismembered branch of the great Appalachian family, and are seen away to the west of the river, swelling up to a noble height, and lording it over the surrounding country. Every change of season, every change of weather, indeed, every hour of the day, produces some change in the magical hues and shapes of these mountains, and they are regarded by all the good wives, far and near, as perfect barometers. When the weather is fair and settled, they are clothed in blue and purple, and print their bold outlines on the clear evening sky; but sometimes, when the rest of the landscape is cloudless, they will gather a hood of grey vapours about their summits, which, in the last rays of the setting sun, will glow and light up like a crown of glory.

—WASHINGTON IRVING, *RIP VAN WINKLE*, 1819

OPPOSITE: Does anyone else hear Carly Simon's "Let the River Run" when they come across a glass-clear creek like this? I want to take my shoes off and wade into a calm inlet, always.

ABOVE: Decorate your lampshades, people. Case in point: this scalloped confection aboard the Venice Simplon Orient Express, stationed in Italy for repair.

In this Virginia horse farm designed by Melinda James, a painted shield-back bench from Palm Beach's Get the Gusto and a custom art rail by the designer give the foyer whiffs of a centuries-old Cumbrian manor.

THE FINE PRINT

◆

Warning: These tips have all the thrill of a trip to the dentist. But in a vacation home at altitude, certain less-than-sexy things are practically required. You'll be wise to consider investing in the following:

Smart Thermostat We had a guest from Texas stay at our mountain house and turn off the thermostat before they checked out, an inadvertent mistake that nearly burst our pipes when the weather turned frigid. Smart thermostats, such as a Nest, can allow you to control a thermostat's heat level from even across the country, so your house never freezes again.

Water Sensors A water sensor that alerts you remotely via text message to possible leaks or flooding, such as SimpliSafe's Water Sensor, can help you have peace of mind when you'll be gone from your property for weeks or months at a time. Tuck them under sinks and by the water heater, dishwasher, washing machine, and more to ensure you're dry.

Boot Trays It's a small thing, but tracks you drag into your alpine abode in mud season can put tears in the eyes of anyone with a mop. Boot trays take up very little real estate on your floor and should be a must next to every entrance to the house.

First Aid Kits We keep first aid kits in our cars and in each bathroom in our mountain house. You never know when you'll need a bandage or ibuprofen, and in this case, the Boy Scouts of America were right: *be prepared.*

Emergency Apps Download apps to your phone that will keep you posted on vital alerts in your area. I personally love the Emergency: Severe Weather App from the American Red Cross, which alerts me to nearby fires, storms, flooding, and more near the locations I choose, so I know when to get out of dodge.

Consider an Induction Stove We have a strict "no flames of any kind" policy at our mountain house, indoors and out. That includes the stove. An electricity-powered induction cooktop can have water at a rapid boil in less than two minutes without heating the surrounding surface.

Satellite Wi-Fi Our internet in the mountains was embarrassingly slow—downright dial-up-y!—until we set up satellite internet with Starlink. Now it's zippy; even faster than it is at our house in the Denver suburbs. Worth every cent.

ABOVE: The craggy sandstone rock formations known as the Flatirons in Boulder, Colorado, are a sacred site for the region's indigenous peoples, including the Ute and Arapaho.

OPPOSITE: For a previously unused room above the garage, the designer Tom Riker convinced his clients to go full throttle on cabin style—cladding the walls in reclaimed barnwood. A rope mirror unearthed at a local antique store; shearling-covered chairs; and the client's own buffalo hide complete the alpine aesthetic.

Windsor Smith HOMEFRONT
FORTUNY
Mrs. Howard Room by Room
BEAUTY AT HOME AERIN LAUDER
LIVING ARCHITECTURE

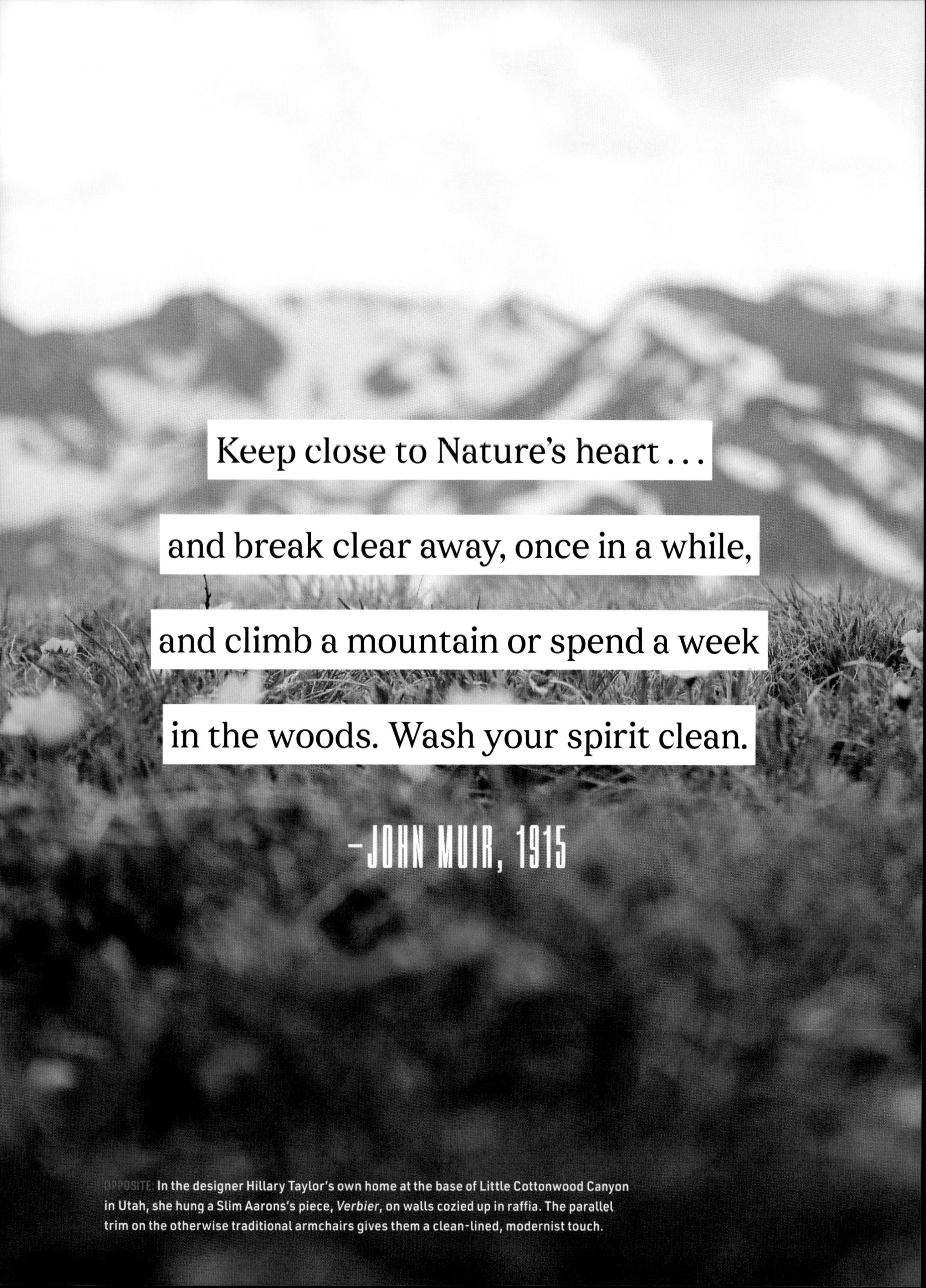

Keep close to Nature's heart . . .

and break clear away, once in a while,

and climb a mountain or spend a week

in the woods. Wash your spirit clean.

—JOHN MUIR, 1915

OPPOSITE: In the designer Hillary Taylor's own home at the base of Little Cottonwood Canyon in Utah, she hung a Slim Aarons's piece, *Verbier*, on walls cozied up in raffia. The parallel trim on the otherwise traditional armchairs gives them a clean-lined, modernist touch.

LEFT: Designer Hillary Taylor's muse for this primary bedroom near Deer Valley, Utah: the woodland decadence of Bavaria. Adding to the effect: the abundant Pierre Frey fabric, La Valliere, which is flat screened on cotton and a pattern original to the nineteenth century.

OPPOSITE: By upholstering the walls of this Utah ranch's media room in Jasper's Indian Flower Fabric, Taylor softened the reclaimed wood ceiling. I love the Scully and Scully sheep ottomans for a note of fun.

SPENBLOCK
NE WAY
rag & bone
NEW YORK
Daniels
Antiques
OLIVELA
CHASE
ELLIOTT YEARY
GALLERY
FINE JEWELRY AND ART
SALE

Adapted from The Little Nell, Aspen, Colorado

The Little Nell is a favorite among bold-faced names for three reasons: its ski-in, ski-out perch at the foot of the Silver Queen Gondola; its après-ski scene at Ajax Tavern; and these flapjacks, which guests have flipped for since the hotel opened the Michelin Guide–recommended Element 47. Lucky for us, the hotel's pastry chefs sent along their recipe.

YIELD: 6 PANCAKES

WET INGREDIENTS

2 eggs, separated

1 cup ricotta cheese

½ cup buttermilk

½ cup butter, melted

1½ teaspoons lemon juice

½ teaspoon vanilla

DRY INGREDIENTS

1 cup cake flour

2 tablespoons all-purpose flour

¼ cup granulated cane sugar

1 teaspoon baking powder

½ teaspoon salt

Dash of nutmeg

Zest of 2 lemons

FOR GARNISH

Powdered sugar

Fresh raspberries

Toasted pine nuts

Beat egg whites until soft peaks form. Combine all dry ingredients together in one bowl, all wet ingredients in another. Gently mix wet ingredients into dry ingredients. Do not overmix batter or pancakes will be dense. Gently fold batter into egg whites.

Heat a large skillet or griddle over medium heat and grease. Spoon 2 to 3 tablespoons of batter onto the skillet and cook until bubbles have formed. Flip and cook the other side until golden brown. Sprinkle with powdered sugar and serve with fresh raspberries and/or garnish with toasted pine nuts, if desired.

Summer

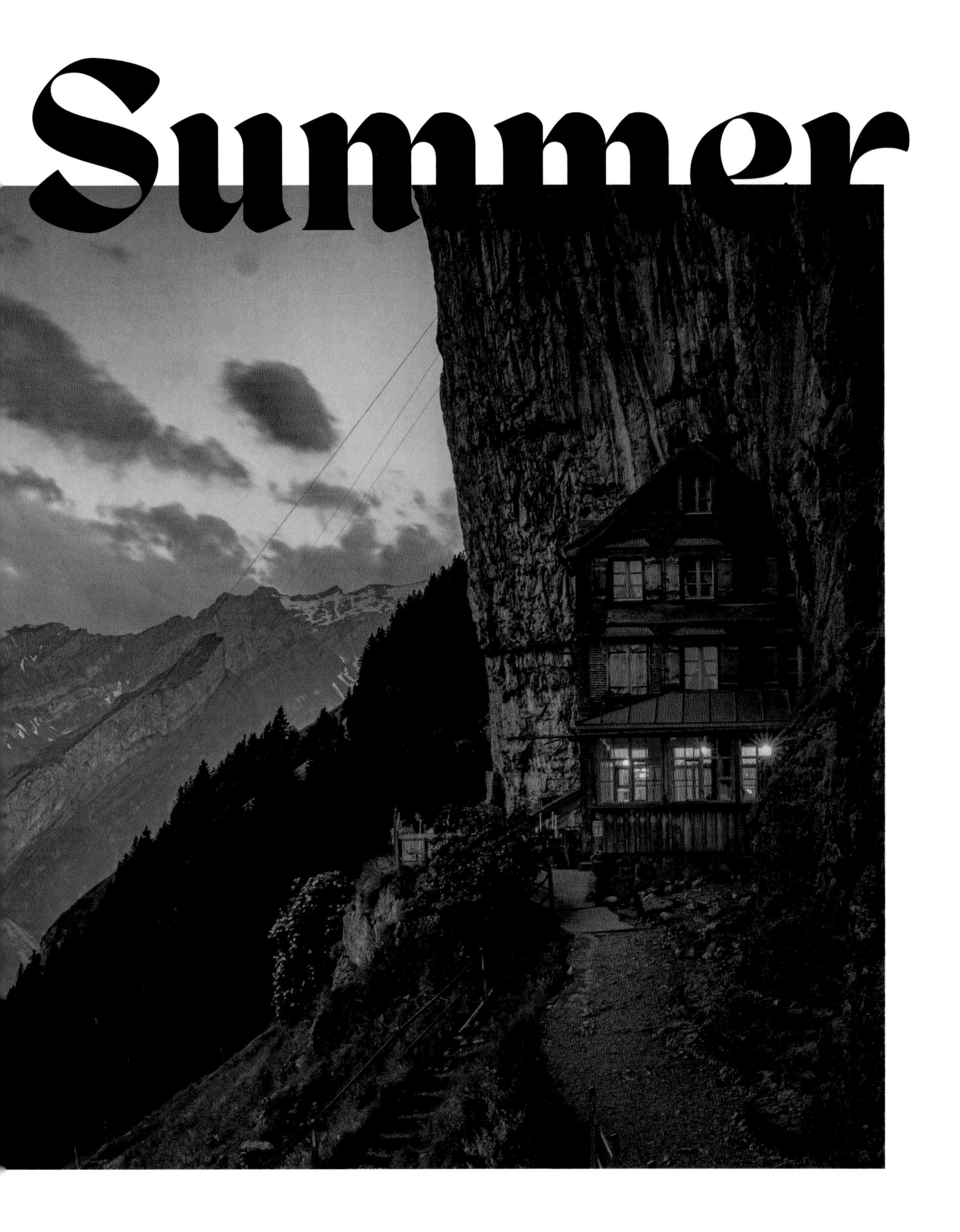

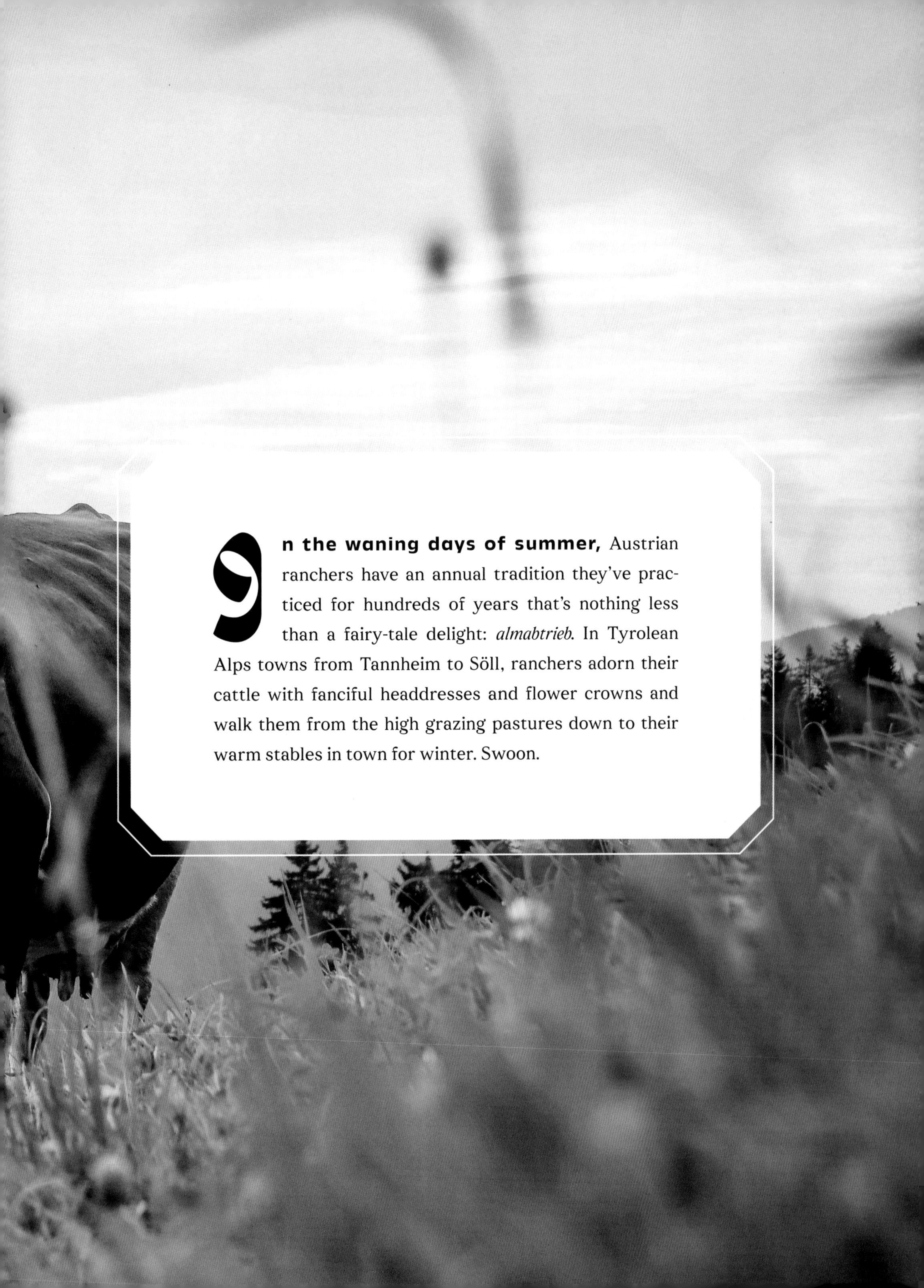

In the waning days of summer, Austrian ranchers have an annual tradition they've practiced for hundreds of years that's nothing less than a fairy-tale delight: *almabtrieb*. In Tyrolean Alps towns from Tannheim to Söll, ranchers adorn their cattle with fanciful headdresses and flower crowns and walk them from the high grazing pastures down to their warm stables in town for winter. Swoon.

HARING
MILES REDD THE BIG BOOK OF CHIC
ALEX KATZ
VICTORIA HAGAN DREAM SPACES
ST. TROPEZ SOLEIL

What I love most about this homecoming custom, besides honoring the animals themselves, is that generations before the advent of Instagram, these farmers indulged in beauty for beauty's sake. That they finish their journey with a festival replete with schnapps and *prügeltorte*—a cake that's layered to bake over a fireside spit—is simply the icing on the *semmelschmarrn*, am I right?

And honestly, doesn't this ritual capture the joy that summer in the mountains is? Swimming in glass-clear lakes, singing around a campfire? And like life itself, always far too short. So in summer it's important to prepare your mountain retreat for an indoor-outdoor lifestyle you can't quite get away with in the depths of winter. The second average daily temperatures hit the 70s, I like to fling open our windows for a good airing out, letting the fresh alpine air work its wizardry. Scrub the cobwebs from your sturdy outdoor chairs and keep throw blankets nearby for stargazing on chilly evenings (a basket inside by the door or locking storage box keeps them out of strong summer breezes but still close).

OPPOSITE: On an eighty-nine-acre ranch on the outskirts of Aspen, architect Celeste Robbins of Robbins Architecture embraced the views—and dreamy light—with floor-to-ceiling glass walls that recede to the alpine air.

ABOVE: Board-formed concrete and wide expanses of glass juxtapose beautifully against the wildness of the Aspen acreage. (The project is featured in Celeste Robbins's book, *The Meaningful Modern Home: Soulful Architecture and Interiors*.)

ABOVE: In the 1970s, Elizabeth Taylor and Richard Burton kept a timbered love-nest chalet in Gstaad. Here in 1955, a young Taylor watercolors the surrounding landscape.

OPPOSITE: Only a clean-lined alfresco pool will do in the mountains; it frames the view. Here, the pool deck by Workshop/APD overlooks the lush and leafy summer Berkshires.

BEAUTY FOR BEAUTY'S SAKE

OPPOSITE: Two tones of wood lend a richness to this Aspen stair hall designed by Robbins Architecture, as seen in Robbins's book, *The Meaningful Modern Home: Soulful Architecture and Interiors*.

ABOVE: Celeste Robbins of Robbins Architecture and team selected sculptural—yet not cloying or colorful—lighting fixtures for this Aspen retreat. Anything else might detract from the land.

I put together a picnic basket with enamel plates, a gingham blanket, flatware, and more, so it's handy for subalpine snacking—just add your favorite foodstuffs, be it queso andino or Gruyère. You may want to freshen up your lake towels and keep them rolled tightly in a woven basket, ready to grab for a last-minute skinny dip. It's also a good idea to invest in those portable outdoor LED lanterns that can last for hours on one charge, maximizing those long summer days.

Inside, hang sheer curtains that softly filter the season's gauzy light, and swap heavier flannels for cotton in a decent thread count. (My secret source for 680 thread count sheets so soft you'll never want to get out of bed? Costco.) Summer is a great time to scour your region's junk shops and flea markets for fresh new tabletop objet—handwoven

LEFT: A table skirt brings some femininity to the wood-on-wood Tennessee mountain powder bath designed by Tammy Connor.

OPPOSITE: The hanging daybed on the screened-in side porch puts lesser outdoor furniture to shame. Tables made from slivers of log nod to the woodsy Tennessee locale.

textiles; or pots thrown in the '70s by a local; or a whittled wonder, like the little wooden fox someone once carved that now stands watch over a side table in our living room at Skytop.

I use the warmer months to excise anything that isn't doing me any favors, simply because clutter is so much easier to get rid of this time of year. And finally, every Memorial Day, be sure to trot out the bikes, kayaks, and other gear from storage and keep them at the ready. The point is to have it all within reach. As we know from an open bag of potato chips sitting on the kitchen counter, anything easily accessed is easily indulged in.

OPPOSITE: Forestis presciently preserved and revamped a 1912 structure on the premises, a commission of the Austrian monarchy.

ABOVE: Flanked by spruce trees, Lago di Carezza is famous for the fortress-like span of the Dolomites that rise behind it and are often reflected in the water. John Singer Sargent painted it in 1914 but called the work by the lake's other name, "Karer See."

SUMMER CHALET TOUR

Telluride, Colorado

◆

The miners that flocked to Telluride during the nineteenth-century gold rush may not have realized the land itself was the real treasure. But the Texas-based designer Linda Eyles did. So when she built the getaway she shares with her husband there, they championed the locale in every way they could—maximizing the views of Little Wasatch mountain and local flora and fauna. (Note the sparrow that appears to alight on the *faux bois* polished brass mirror.)

OPPOSITE: For her terrace set under the Wasatch Mountains, Eyles opted for stackable chairs that could quickly be tucked into storage at the end of the summer.

ABOVE: Slatted blonde wood walls separate living spaces while allowing daylight to flow in designer Linda Eyles's Telluride, Colorado, getaway home.

SOREL
SOREL

PREVIOUS: A touch of faux bois—in the bathroom's mirror and the door handle—can make any room feel more at one with nature.

OPPOSITE: White-oak paneled walls and concrete floors stand up to ski boots and muddy dog paws alike in the entrance hall.

ABOVE: To maximize real estate, Eyles built a bar setup just below the stairs in a guest wing and painted the cabinetry Benjamin Moore's Blue Danube. The art piece is by Aondrea Maynard.

PREVIOUS: Preserving oak trees that had stood for decades on this plot in the foothills of California's Santa Ynez Mountains was vital for Brandon Architects and Patterson Custom Homes. They made multiple site visits to ensure that—all worth it for the views out these glass walls.

OPPOSITE: The exterior tumbled palomino limestone feels historic, especially paired with Western red cedar and stucco; but the walls of iron windows will always look modern.

ABOVE: Ceramic lamps bring the hand of the artisan in in a way that always feels authentic in the wilderness. Linen duvet covers and a rough wood bench supply earthiness, too.

ABOVE: Why not build your own swimming hole? This one has an infinity edge that puts the focus on the surrounding landscape.

OPPOSITE: Stone walls will always feel ancient and Old World, even when they've just been built. (These tumbled palomino limestones were selected by Brandon Architects, stone by stone.)

LEFT: Rift sawn oak cabinets, pendant lamps with brass interiors, and glimmery zellige tile warm up the otherwise sleek open cookspace by Brandon Architects.

OPPOSITE: At twilight, the barn by Brandon Architects—which is set about a mile from the main house, and contains a bar and game room—feels like a portal to another, slower time.

The inky black tiles under the barn's bar, designed by Brandon Architects, glimmer by day and night.

Mountains of MONOGRAMS

◆

Nothing seems more out of place in a mountain house than a monogram, a more common hallmark of Southern houses and East Coast prep. Or is it? A ranch often has its own brand, even if they don't have cattle; the symbol is used on gates and equipment so you know at a glance you've arrived. Padlock Ranch in Wyoming uses the symbol of an open lock; Texas's 825,000-acre King Ranch has used a curvaceous "running W" as its brand since 1869. If you'd like a custom monogram or brand symbol but you're not a graphic designer, reach out to one on Etsy to design one for you. Then have your chosen brand emblazoned on everything from cocktail napkins to mugs, throw blankets to beanie hats (websites like Zazzle make it easy). It will remind you of your cherished mountain home wherever you roam.

Varied taper heights and abundant Pendleton blankets create a swoon-inducing tablescape for a wedding at Dunton River Camp, a five-hundred-acre retreat on a former cattle ranch perched on the West Fork of the Dolores River in Dolores, Colorado.

ABOVE: There's a grandness to the wide gable of Verbier's Experimental Chalet that recalls the wingspan of a golden eagle.

LEFT: Fling your windows open to the alpine air as much as possible in summer, or you may regret it in the stuffy days of winter.

Adapted from the Restaurant at the Chedi Andermatt, Andermatt, Switzerland

The Chedi Andermatt looks as if Heidi's storybook chalet swallowed Alice in Wonderland's pill. They serve their bison entrecôte (rib eye) at the height of summer—what better dish to fuel the day's exploits? I suggest going for a rib eye that is local to you, be it buffalo or bovine.

YIELD: 6 SERVINGS

2½ pounds potatoes, such as Yukon Golds

¾ cup beurre noisette, or browned unsalted butter (recipe below)

Sea salt

Salt

2¼ pounds bison (or beef) entrecôte (rib-eye cut)

12 precooked pearl onions

1 tablespoon butter

1 tablespoon brown sugar

Black pepper

Fresh truffles

FOR THE BÉARNAISE

¼ cup white wine vinegar

½ cup dry white wine

1 finely chopped shallot

2 egg yolks

6 tablespoons cold butter, cut in pieces

1 sprig of tarragon, finely chopped

Preheat the oven to 350°F. To make the *beurre noisette*, or brown butter, melt unsalted butter over low heat and allow it to separate into butterfat and milk solids. The latter naturally sinks to the bottom of the pan and will begin to turn a deep brown. When it reaches a toasty hazelnut hue, remove the pan from heat.

Peel the potatoes and cut into thin slices. Mix the *beurre noisette* and salt to taste into the potato slices. Line a loaf pan with baking paper and layer the potato slices one after the other and bake in the oven for about 1 hour.

After cooking, weigh down the potatoes with a layer of parchment under another pot so that everything is nicely compressed, then leave to rest in the refrigerator for 8 hours to firm. After hardening, cut into rectangles and fry in a pan until golden brown, and then bake in the oven at 350°F for 10 minutes.

Sear the bison entrecôte for 1 minute on both sides and then cook until pink in the center at 350°F in a convection oven for 15 to 20 minutes. Briefly sauté the precooked pearl onions in butter and brown sugar and caramelize.

For the béarnaise, in a small chrome steel pan, combine the white wine vinegar, white wine, shallot, and salt and bring to a boil; reduce heat and simmer until reduced to 2 tablespoons. Strain, then pour the liquid back into the pan or into a chrome steel bowl. Stir the egg yolks into the reduction (sifted liquid). Beat in a water bath at 175°F to form an airy, creamy mass. Add the butter while stirring until the sauce is creamy. Remove from the water bath, stir in the tarragon, and season to taste with salt and pepper.

To serve, for each plate, start with the potato rectangle and place 2 pearl onions on top. Cut the bison entrecôte into slices and add 1 tablespoon of béarnaise sauce and grate the truffles over it.

OPPOSITE: In photographer Lisa Flood's primary bedroom, the window treatments tucked under the exposed beams are Antoinette Poisson's Jaipur fabric, a find from Janak and Flood's trip to Paris for shopping and inspiration.

ABOVE: To bring a note of France into Flood's Wyoming cabin, Jackson Hole designer Emily Janak used Pierre Frey wallcovering in the stair hall. The antique hat stand is by Old Hickory, which was founded in 1899.

ABOVE: One of photographer Lisa Flood's interests—collecting antique cowboy hats—served Janak beautifully in the decoration of her Wyoming home. Even piled atop a bench, they add texture and the unbridled aura of the region.

OPPOSITE: I like to keep bedside tables spare and uncluttered. This is styled perfectly, with its nosegay of fresh flowers and small stack of tomes curated by Foxtail Books & Library Services.

WILDFLOWER Arranging 101

◆

Just beyond the doors of Skytop Mountain House in Bailey, Colorado, each summer, a de facto rainbow springs from the earth: silvery lupine in shades of lavender and lilac; the scruffy pink Eaton's thistle and bridal-white common yarrow; and pincushion beardtongue that stands regal and indigo blue. They're scragglier than the imported blooms you'll find at the flower market but that's part of their appeal—especially when you juxtapose them in a modern vase. Here, how to make the best of stems plucked on your private property so you can enjoy the fruits of the summer indoors and out:

Keep It Tonal I find unruly florals often look better when kept within different shades of one singular color—sky blues, sunset pinks, or the pure white of a fresh snowfall.

Use a (Heavy) Flower Frog In nature, especially, I prefer to avoid toss-away flower-arranging materials like floral foam in favor of something that lasts year after year. Flower frogs reportedly originated in fourteenth-century Japan and are still useful today for buttressing stems from flopping over. I like that they make arranging in even the shallowest dishes and bowls doable.

Freshen Them Up Change the water every day and, if you'll be away a night or two, stick your bouquet in the fridge. Once wildflowers are past their prime, I scatter their seedheads back in nature rather than dumping them in a landfill. We are dust, and to dust we shall return.

Janak arranged vintage saddle stools around the table in photographer Lisa Flood's Wyoming home. The dresser is a Welsh heirloom that Flood inherited from her grandmother and stocked with antique Yellowstone National Park plates.

From the terrace of the Tower Suite at Forestis, the Dolomites are the most delightful mountain neighbor one could have: quiet and awe-inducing.

All the beauty and glory are but the frame out of which rises—heaven-piercing, pure in its pearly luster, as glorious a mountain as the sun tinges red in either hemisphere—the splintered, pinnacled, lonely, ghastly, imposing, double-peaked summit of Long's Peak, the Mont Blanc of Northern Colorado.

—ISABELLA BIRD, *A LADY'S LIFE IN THE ROCKY MOUNTAINS*, 1879

CREDITS

◆

Slim Aarons/Getty Images: 4
Slim Aarons/Hulton Archive/Getty Images: 14
Atosan/shutterstock.com: 66
Engin Akyurt/Unsplash.com: 215 background
Clay Banks/Unsplash.com: 123 background
Fokke Baarssen/shutterstock.com: 181
Jenelle Ball/Unsplash.com: 1
Jane Beiles: 92
Simon Berger/Unsplash.com: 118 background
Simon Berger/Unsplash.com: 179
Nicolai Berntsen/Unsplash.com: 18
biletskiyevgeniy.com/shutterstock.com: 41
Kristi Blokhin/shutterstock.com: 178
Francis Bouffard/Unsplash.com: 112
Taylor Brandon/Unsplash.com: 172
Valentin Chrétien/Unsplash.com: 12
Michael P.H. Clifford: 132–35
Robert Crum/shutterstock.com: 186 background
Tony Dearwester/Unsplash.com: 88 background
Deman/shutterstock.com: 72 right
Bea de Ros/Unsplash.com: 121
Bernd Dittrich/Unsplash.com: 6
Greg Duprat/Unsplash.com: 18–19 background
Shannon Dupre': 98–103, 140–41
Aleksandr Emelianov/shutterstock.com: 220
Jessica Fadel/Unsplash.com: 175
Filippo.P/shutterstock.com: 169
Film Publicity Archive/United Archives via Getty Images: 13
Ben Finch, Finch Photography: 64–65
Terry Fincher/Getty Images: 80
Lisa Flood: 68–71, 116–19, 161–65, 216–18, 221
Courtesy Forestis: 94–95, 194–195, 222–225
Courtesy Naturhotel Forsthofgut: 82–87
Gado/Getty Images: 16
Kimberly Gavin: 38, 142–42
Judith Girard Marczak/Unsplash.com: 17
Elinda Gjonomadhi/Unsplash.com: 15
Alberto Garcia Guillen/shutterstock.com: 131
Scott Hall: 42–47, 184–85, 188–91
Toa Heftiba/unsplash.com: front cover
Courtesy Hotel Jerome, Auberge Resorts Collection: 77
Michael Hunter: 67
Hans Isaacson/Unsplash.com: 122
iSidhe/iStock.com: spine, 166
Gaspar Janos/shutterstock.com: 146
Quenten Janssen/Unsplash.com: 90
Joyfull/shutterstock.com: 10–11, 124
Anna Kaminova/Unsplash.com: 76
Whitney Kamman: 136, 173
Pawel Kazmierczak/shutterstock.com: 107

Younès Klouche, courtesy Drei Berge Hotel: back cover, 2–3, 147–55
Igor Kovalchuk/shutterstock.com: 23
Manolo Langis: 25, 202–11
Aaron Leitz: 28
Marina Litvinova/shutterstock.com: 180
Tony Litvyak/Unsplash.com: 126
Lizavetta/shutterstock.com: 166
Patrick Locqueneux, courtesy Le Coucou: 48–55
Patrick Locqueneux, courtesy Experimental Chalet: 156–58
Alexandra Luniel/Unsplash.com: 78
Austin Mann, courtesy Dunton Hot Springs: 34
Sonny Mauricio/Unsplash.com: 171
Andrew Mayovskyy/shutterstock.com: 26
melissamn/shutterstock.com: 168
Michel Reybier Hospitality, courtesy Mont Cervin Palace: 138–39
Milles Studio/shutterstock.com: 72 left
Karyn Millet: 74–75
Anna Nahabed/shutterstock.com: 125
Heather Nan: 174
Nevels Media/Unsplash.com: 160
Svetlana Orusova/shutterstock.com: 130
Kathryn O'Shea-Evans: 13, 21, 62, 105
Pandora Pictures/shutterstock.com: 22
PangJee_S/shutterstock.com: 159
Peter116/shutterstock.com: 24
Peter_C/shutterstock.com: 29
Robert Peterson: 88
Eric Piasecki/OTTO: 30, 31, 36, 108–9, 114–15, 144–45, 192–93
Joel Pitra: 187
PLG/iStock.com: 166
Dino Reichmuth/Unsplash.com: 2-3
Robert Reyes/Unsplash.com: 40
Jack Richmond, courtesy Dunton Hot Springs: 32, 96–97, 212–13
Angela Roy: 60–61, 110–11, 120, 128–29, 170
rybarmarekk/shutterstock.com: 113
salilbhatt/shutterstock.com: 176–77 bottom
Nathan Schroder: 176–77
Schumacher: Endpapers, 62–63, 117, 137, 163
Stephan Seeber/Unsplash.com: 182
SeregaSibTravel/shutterstock.com: 36
Kelly Sikkema/Unsplash.com: 89
Silver Screen Collection/Getty Images: 186
Smit/shutterstock.com: 79
Julie Soefer: 196–201
Songtam Srinakarin/shutterstock.com: 232
Zoltan Tasi/Unsplash.com: 105
Mr. Tripper, courtesy Experimental Chalet: 56–59, 127, 156, 158, 214, 229, 230
Unomat/iStock.com: 34, 107
Artiom Vallat/Unsplash.com: 22–23 center
Konstantin Volkmar: 93–95, 194–95, 222–25
Kevin Wenning/Unsplash.com: 8
Vladimir Wrangel/shutterstock.com: 20
Peter Zenkl/iStock.com: 123

ACKNOWLEDGMENTS

◆

If you're going to plop a house or hotel amid an untrammeled natural landscape, you'd better make it beautiful. The interior designers and architects whose work is featured in this book have achieved just that. So I'd like to begin by thanking all of the aesthetic wizards who brought alpine dreams to life in the structures within these pages. To the photographers (listed page 226) who were so kind and generous with their work, *thank you*. You capture life and light in lovely ways, #nofilter needed. To the team at Gibbs Smith, especially my dazzling editor, Juree Sondker: you're a visionary and a total delight. For book designers Amy Sly and Ryan Thomann: thank you for not laughing when I said I wanted this book to look like a fairy tale, and for making that idea come to be—happily ever after. And, finally thank you to all my parents, who gave me my love of natural beauty, good design and books—or better yet, a combo of all three, plus snacks—from the start.

MONOPOLY
500
Hasbro Gaming
GEHE 3 FELDER ZURÜCK.
AARAU RATHAUSPLATZ
CHANCE
NEUENBURG PLACE PURY
NEUCHÂTEL PLACE PURY
THUN HAUPTGASSE
THOUNE HAUPTGASSE
ELEKTRIZITÄTSWERKE
USINES ÉLECTRIQUES
BASEL STEINEN-VORSTADT
BÂLE STEINEN-VORSTADT
IM GEFÄNGNIS
EN PRISON
NUR ZU BESUCH
SIMPLE VISITE
Das berühmte Spiel um de
Le jeu des transactions immo
AMIMO
KIDS

BIO

◆

Kathryn O'Shea-Evans writes about design, travel, and food from her home base in Colorado's Front Range. A graduate of Harvard University's Extension School and contributing editor at *House Beautiful* magazine, her writing has appeared in *The Wall Street Journal*, *The New York Times*, and *The Washington Post*.